BY THE SAME AUTHOR

INDIAN CURRENCY AND FINANCE.
Pp. viii + 263. 1913.
7s. 6d. (5th thousand.)

THE ECONOMIC CONSEQUENCES OF
THE PEACE.
Pp. vii + 279. 1919.
8s. 6d. (84th thousand.)

A TREATISE ON PROBABILITY.
Pp. xi + 466. 1921.
18s. (3rd thousand.)

A REVISION OF THE TREATY.
Pp. viii + 223. 1922.
7s. 6d. (13th thousand.)

A TRACT ON MONETARY REFORM.
Pp. viii + 209. 1923.
7s. 6d. (12th thousand.)

A TREATISE ON MONEY.
Vol. I.—Pp. xvii + 363. 1930.
Vol. II.—Pp. viii + 424. 1930.
15s. each. (7th thousand.)

ESSAYS IN PERSUASION.
Pp. xiii + 376. 1931.
10s. 6d. (8th thousand.)
Popular Edition. 1933.
5s.

THE MEANS TO PROSPERITY.
Pp. 40. 1933.
1s. (13th thousand.)

(The figures of sales are for Great Britain and
the United States, exclusive of translations.)

ESSAYS IN BIOGRAPHY

MACMILLAN AND CO., Limited
LONDON · BOMBAY · CALCUTTA · MADRAS
MELBOURNE

ESSAYS
IN
BIOGRAPHY

BY

JOHN MAYNARD KEYNES

FELLOW OF KING'S COLLEGE, CAMBRIDGE

MACMILLAN AND CO., LIMITED
ST. MARTIN'S STREET, LONDON
1933

PRINTED IN GREAT BRITAIN
BY R. & R. CLARK, LIMITED, EDINBURGH

PREFACE

WITH two or three obvious exceptions, these essays are based on direct acquaintance. Most of them were composed under the immediate impression of the characters described. They are offered to the reader (except in the case of the essay on Robert Malthus) as being of this nature—not written coolly, long afterwards, in the perspective of history. The essays on Mr. Lloyd George and on Robert Malthus have not been published previously. References to the sources of the other essays are given in an appendix.

In the second section some scattered commentary will be found on the history and progress of economic doctrine; though my main purpose has been biographical. Incidentally, I have sought with some touches of detail to bring out the solidarity and historical continuity of the High Intelligentsia of England, who have built up the foundations of our thought in the two and a half centuries, since Locke, in his *Essay*

vii

Concerning Human Understanding, wrote the first modern English book. I relate below (p. 82) the amazing progeny of Sir George Villiers. But the lineage of the High Intelligentsia is hardly less interbred and spiritually intermixed. Let the Villiers Connection fascinate the monarch or the mob and rule, or seem to rule, passing events. There is also a pride of sentiment to claim spiritual kinship with the Locke Connection and that long English line, intellectually and humanly linked with one another, to which the names in my second section belong. If not the wisest, yet the most truthful of men. If not the most personable, yet the queerest and sweetest. If not the most practical, yet of the purest public conscience. If not of high artistic genius, yet of the most solid and sincere accomplishment within many of the fields which are ranged by the human mind.

J. M. KEYNES

KING'S COLLEGE, CAMBRIDGE,
February 1933.

I have taken the opportunity of a reprint of this book to make a few minor corrections, mainly in the references to Malthus's living on p. 113, and to the Edgeworth family in the footnotes on p. 267.

J. M. K.

April 1933.

CONTENTS

I. SKETCHES OF POLITICIANS

II. LIVES OF ECONOMISTS

(Dedicated to Mary Paley Marshall)

PLATES

I
SKETCHES OF POLITICIANS

THE COUNCIL OF FOUR, PARIS, 1919

CLEMENCEAU was by far the most eminent member of the Council of Four, and he had taken the measure of his colleagues. He alone both had an idea and had considered it in all its consequences. His age, his character, his wit, and his appearance joined to give him objectivity and a defined outline in an environment of confusion. One could not despise Clemenceau or dislike him, but only take a different view as to the nature of civilised man, or indulge, at least, a different hope.

The figure and bearing of Clemenceau are universally familiar. At the Council of Four he wore a square-tailed coat of very good, thick black broadcloth, and on his hands, which were never uncovered, grey suède gloves; his boots were of thick black leather, very good, but of a country style, and sometimes fastened in front, curiously, by a buckle instead of laces. His seat in the room in the President's house, where the regular meetings of the Council of Four were held (as distinguished from their

private and unattended conferences in a smaller
chamber below), was on a square brocaded
chair in the middle of the semicircle facing the
fire-place, with Signor Orlando on his left, the
President next by the fire-place, and the Prime
Minister opposite on the other side of the fire-
place on his right.   He carried no papers and
no portfolio, and was unattended by any personal
secretary, though several French ministers and
officials appropriate to the particular matter in
hand would be present round him.   His walk,
his hand, and his voice were not lacking in
vigour, but he bore, nevertheless, especially
after the attempt upon him, the aspect of a very
old man conserving his strength for important
occasions.   He spoke seldom, leaving the
initial statement of the French case to his
ministers or officials; he closed his eyes often
and sat back in his chair with an impassive face
of parchment, his grey-gloved hands clasped in
front of him.   A short sentence, decisive or
cynical, was generally sufficient, a question, an
unqualified abandonment of his ministers, whose
face would not be saved, or a display of obstinacy reinforced by a few words in a piquantly
delivered English.[1]   But speech and passion

[1] He alone amongst the Four could speak and understand both
languages, Orlando knowing only French and the Prime Minister
and the President only English; and it is of historical importance that
Orlando and the President had no direct means of communication.

were not lacking when they were wanted, and the sudden outburst of words, often followed by a fit of deep coughing from the chest, produced their impression rather by force and surprise than by persuasion.

Not infrequently, Mr. Lloyd George, after delivering a speech in English, would, during the period of its interpretation into French, cross the hearthrug to the President to reinforce his case by some *ad hominem* argument in private conversation, or to sound the ground for a compromise—and this would sometimes be the signal for a general upheaval and disorder. The President's advisers would press round him, a moment later the British experts would dribble across to learn the result or see that all was well, and next the French would be there, a little suspicious lest the others were arranging something behind them, until all the room were on their feet and conversation was general in both languages. My last and most vivid impression is of such a scene—the President and the Prime Minister as the centre of a surging mob and a babel of sound, a welter of eager, impromptu compromises and counter-compromises, all sound and fury signifying nothing, on what was an unreal question anyhow, the great issues of the morning's meeting forgotten and neglected; and Clemenceau, silent and aloof on the out-

skirts—for nothing which touched the security
of France was forward—throned, in his grey
gloves, on the brocade chair, dry in soul and
empty of hope, very old and tired, but surveying
the scene with a cynical and almost impish air;
and when at last silence was restored and the
company had returned to their places, it was to
discover that he had disappeared.

He felt about France what Pericles felt of
Athens—unique value in her, nothing else
mattering; but his theory of politics was Bis-
marck's. He had one illusion—France; and
one disillusion—mankind, including French-
men and his colleagues not least. His principles for the Peace can be expressed simply.
In the first place, he was a foremost believer in
the view of German psychology that the German
understands and can understand nothing but
intimidation, that he is without generosity or
remorse in negotiation, that there is no advantage he will not take of you, and no extent to
which he will not demean himself for profit,
that he is without honour, pride, or mercy.
Therefore you must never negotiate with a
German or conciliate him; you must dictate to
him. On no other terms will he respect you,
or will you prevent him from cheating you.
But it is doubtful how far he thought these
characteristics peculiar to Germany, or whether

his candid view of some other nations was fundamentally different. His philosophy had, therefore, no place for "sentimentality" in international relations. Nations are real things, of which you love one and feel for the rest indifference—or hatred. The glory of the nation you love is a desirable end—but generally to be obtained at your neighbour's expense. The politics of power are inevitable, and there is nothing very new to learn about this war or the end it was fought for; England had destroyed, as in each preceding century, a trade rival; a mighty chapter had been closed in the secular struggle between the glories of Germany and of France. Prudence required some measure of lip service to the "ideals" of foolish Americans and hypocritical Englishmen; but it would be stupid to believe that there is much room in the world, as it really is, for such affairs as the League of Nations, or any sense in the principle of self-determination except as an ingenious formula for rearranging the balance of power in one's own interests.

These, however, are generalities. In tracing the practical details of the Peace which he thought necessary for the power and the security of France, we must go back to the historical causes which had operated during his lifetime. Before the Franco-German war the populations

of France and Germany were approximately
equal; but the coal and iron and shipping of
Germany were in their infancy and the wealth
of France was greatly superior. Even after
the loss of Alsace-Lorraine there was no great
discrepancy between the real resources of the
two countries. But in the intervening period
the relative position had changed completely.
By 1914 the population of Germany was nearly
70 per cent in excess of that of France; she had
become one of the first manufacturing and
trading nations of the world; her technical skill
and her means for the production of future
wealth were unequalled. France, on the other
hand, had a stationary or declining population,
and, relatively to others, had fallen seriously
behind in wealth and in the power to produce it.

In spite, therefore, of France's victorious
issue from the present struggle (with the aid,
this time, of England and America), her future
position remained precarious in the eyes of one
who took the view that European civil war is to
be regarded as a normal, or at least a recurrent,
state of affairs for the future, and that the sort
of conflicts between organised Great Powers
which have occupied the past hundred years will
also engage the next. According to this vision
of the future, European history is to be a perpetual prize-fight, of which France has won this

round, but of which this round is certainly not the last. From the belief that essentially the old order does not change, being based on human nature which is always the same, and from a consequent scepticism of all that class of doctrine which the League of Nations stands for, the policy of France and of Clemenceau followed logically. For a Peace of magnanimity or of fair and equal treatment, based on such "ideology" as the Fourteen Points of the President, could only have the effect of shortening the interval of Germany's recovery and hastening the day when she will once again hurl at France her greater numbers and her superior resources and technical skill. Hence the necessity of "guarantees"; and each guarantee that was taken, by increasing irritation and thus the probability of a subsequent *revanche* by Germany, made necessary yet further provisions to crush. Thus, as soon as this view of the world is adopted and the other discarded, a demand for a Carthaginian Peace is inevitable, to the full extent of the momentary power to impose it. For Clemenceau made no pretence of considering himself bound by the Fourteen Points, and left chiefly to others such concoctions as were necessary from time to time to save the scruples or the face of the President.

So far as possible, therefore, it was the policy

of France to set the clock back and to undo what, since 1870, the progress of Germany had accomplished. By loss of territory and other measures her population was to be curtailed; but chiefly the economic system, upon which she depended for her new strength, the vast fabric built upon iron, coal, and transport, must be destroyed. If France could seize, even in part, what Germany was compelled to drop, the inequality of strength between the two rivals for European hegemony might be remedied for many generations. Hence sprang those cumulative provisions of the Treaty for the destruction of highly organised economic life.

This is the policy of an old man, whose most vivid impressions and most lively imagination are of the past and not of the future. He sees the issue in terms of France and Germany, not of humanity and of European civilisation struggling forwards to a new order. The war has bitten into his consciousness somewhat differently from ours, and he neither expects nor hopes that we are at the threshold of a new age.

It happens, however, that it is not only an ideal question that is at issue. The Carthaginian Peace is not *practically* right or possible. Although the school of thought from which it springs is aware of the economic factor, it overlooks, nevertheless, the deeper economic tendencies which are to govern the future. The clock cannot be set back. You cannot restore Central Europe to 1870 without setting up such strains in the European structure and letting loose such human and spiritual forces as, pushing beyond frontiers and races, will overwhelm not only you and your "guarantees," but your institutions, and the existing order of your Society.

By what legerdemain was this policy substituted for the Fourteen Points, and how did the President come to accept it? The answer to these questions is difficult and depends on elements of character and psychology and on the subtle influence of surroundings, which are hard to detect and harder still to describe. But, if ever the action of a single individual matters, the collapse of the President has been one of the decisive moral events of history; and I must make an attempt to explain it. What a place the President held in the hearts and hopes of the world when he sailed to us in the *George Washington*! What a great man came to Europe in those early days of our victory!

In November 1918 the armies of Foch and the words of Wilson had brought us sudden escape from what was swallowing up all we cared for. The conditions seemed favourable beyond any expectation. The victory was so complete that fear need play no part in the settlement. The enemy had laid down his arms in reliance on a solemn compact as to the general character of the Peace, the terms of which seemed to assure a settlement of justice and magnanimity and a fair hope for a restoration of the broken current of life. To make assurance certain the President was coming himself to set the seal on his work.

When President Wilson left Washington he enjoyed a prestige and a moral influence throughout the world unequalled in history. His bold and measured words carried to the peoples of Europe above and beyond the voices of their own politicians. The enemy peoples trusted him to carry out the compact he had made with them; and the allied peoples acknowledged him not as a victor only but almost as a prophet. In addition to this moral influence, the realities of power were in his hands. The American armies were at the height of their numbers, discipline, and equipment. Europe was in complete dependence on the food supplies of the United States; and financially she was even more absolutely at their mercy. Europe not only already owed the United States more than she could pay; but only a large measure of further assistance could save her from starvation and bankruptcy. Never had a philosopher held such weapons wherewith to bind the princes of this world. How the crowds of the European capitals pressed about the carriage of the President! With what curiosity, anxiety, and hope we sought a glimpse of the features and bearing of the man of destiny who, coming from the West, was to bring healing to the wounds of the ancient parent of his civilisation and lay for us the foundations of the future.

The disillusion was so complete that some of those who had trusted most hardly dared speak of it. Could it be true? they asked of those who returned from Paris. Was the Treaty really as bad as it seemed? What had happened to the President? What weakness or what misfortune had led to so extraordinary, so unlooked-for a betrayal?

Yet the causes were very ordinary and human. The President was not a hero or a prophet; he was not even a philosopher; but a generously intentioned man, with many of the weaknesses of other human beings, and lacking that dominating intellectual equipment which would have been necessary to cope with the subtle and dangerous spell-binders whom a tremendous clash of forces and personalities had brought to the top as triumphant masters in the swift game

of give and take, face to face in Council—a
game of which he had no experience at all.

We had indeed quite a wrong idea of the
President. We knew him to be solitary and
aloof, and believed him very strong-willed and
obstinate. We did not figure him as a man of
detail, but the clearness with which he had
taken hold of certain main ideas would, we
thought, in combination with his tenacity, en-
able him to sweep through cobwebs. Besides
these qualities he would have the objectivity,
the cultivation, and the wide knowledge of the
student. The great distinction of language
which had marked his famous Notes seemed to
indicate a man of lofty and powerful imagination. His portraits indicated a fine presence
and a commanding delivery. With all this he
had attained and held with increasing authority
the first position in a country where the arts of
the politician are not neglected. All of which,
without expecting the impossible, seemed a fine
combination of qualities for the matter in hand.

The first impression of Mr. Wilson at close
quarters was to impair some but not all of these
illusions. His head and features were finely
cut and exactly like his photographs, and the
muscles of his neck and the carriage of his head
were distinguished. But, like Odysseus, the
President looked wiser when he was seated;

and his hands, though capable and fairly strong,
were wanting in sensitiveness and finesse.   The
first glance at the President suggested not only
that, whatever else he might be, his temperament was not primarily that of the student or
the scholar, but that he had not much even of
that culture of the world which marks M.
Clemenceau and Mr. Balfour as exquisitely
cultivated gentlemen of their class and generation.   But more serious than this, he was not
only insensitive to his surroundings in the
external sense, he was not sensitive to his
environment at all.   What chance could such a
man have against Mr. Lloyd George's unerring,
almost medium-like, sensibility to everyone
immediately round him?   To see the British
Prime Minister watching the company, with
six or seven senses not available to ordinary
men, judging character, motive, and subconscious impulse, perceiving what each was
thinking and even what each was going to say
next, and compounding with telepathic instinct
the argument or appeal best suited to the vanity,
weakness, or self-interest of his immediate
auditor, was to realise that the poor President
would be playing blind-man's-buff in that party.
Never could a man have stepped into the parlour
a more perfect and predestined victim to the
finished accomplishments of the Prime Minister.

The Old World was tough in wickedness, anyhow; the Old World's heart of stone might
blunt the sharpest blade of the bravest knight-
errant.   But this blind and deaf Don Quixote
was entering a cavern where the swift and
glittering blade was in the hands of the adversary.

But if the President was not the philosopher-
king, what was he?   After all, he was a man
who had spent much of his life at a University.
He was by no means a business man or an
ordinary party politician, but a man of force,
personality, and importance.   What, then, was
his temperament?

The clue, once found, was illuminating.   The
President was like a Nonconformist minister,
perhaps a Presbyterian.   His thought and his
temperament were essentially theological, not
intellectual, with all the strength and the weakness of that manner of thought, feeling, and
expression.   It is a type of which there are not
now in England and Scotland such magnificent
specimens as formerly; but this description,
nevertheless, will give the ordinary Englishman
the distinctest impression of the President.

With this picture of him in mind we can
return to the actual course of events.   The
President's programme for the world, as set
forth in his speeches and his Notes, had dis-

played a spirit and a purpose so admirable that the last desire of his sympathisers was to criticise details—the details, they felt, were quite rightly not filled in at present, but would be in due course. It was commonly believed at the commencement of the Paris Conference that the President had thought out, with the aid of a large body of advisers, a comprehensive scheme not only for the League of Nations but for the embodiment of the Fourteen Points in an actual Treaty of Peace. But in fact the President had thought out nothing; when it came to practice, his ideas were nebulous and incomplete. He had no plan, no scheme, no constructive ideas whatever for clothing with the flesh of life the commandments which he had thundered from the White House. He could have preached a sermon on any of them or have addressed a stately prayer to the Almighty for their fulfilment, but he could not frame their concrete application to the actual state of Europe.

He not only had no proposals in detail, but he was in many respects, perhaps inevitably, ill-informed as to European conditions. And not only was he ill-informed—that was true of Mr. Lloyd George also—but his mind was slow and unadaptable. The President's slowness amongst the Europeans was noteworthy. He could not, all in a minute, take in what the

c

rest were saying, size up the situation with a
glance, frame a reply, and meet the case by a
slight change of ground; and he was liable,
therefore, to defeat by the mere swiftness,
apprehension, and agility of a Lloyd George.
There can seldom have been a statesman of the
first rank more incompetent than the President
in the agilities of the council chamber. A
moment often arrives when substantial victory
is yours if by some slight appearance of a concession you can save the face of the opposition
or conciliate them by a restatement of your
proposal helpful to them and not injurious to
anything essential to yourself. The President
was not equipped with this simple and usual
artfulness. His mind was too slow and un-
resourceful to be ready with *any* alternatives.
The President was capable of digging his toes
in and refusing to budge, as he did over Fiume.
But he had no other mode of defence, and it
needed as a rule but little manœuvring by his
opponents to prevent matters from coming to
such a head until it was too late. By pleasant-
ness and an appearance of conciliation the
President would be manœuvred off his ground,
would miss the moment for digging his toes in,
and, before he knew where he had been got to,
it was too late. Besides, it is impossible month
after month in intimate and ostensibly friendly

converse between close associates to be digging the toes in all the time. Victory would only have been possible to one who had always a sufficiently lively apprehension of the position as a whole to reserve his fire and know for certain the rare exact moments for decisive action. And for that the President was far too slow-minded and bewildered.

He did not remedy these defects by seeking aid from the collective wisdom of his lieutenants. He had gathered round him for the economic chapters of the Treaty a very able group of business men; but they were inexperienced in public affairs and knew (with one or two exceptions) as little of Europe as he did, and they were only called in irregularly as he might need them for a particular purpose. Thus the aloofness which had been found effective in Washington was maintained, and the abnormal reserve of his nature did not allow near him anyone who aspired to moral equality or the continuous exercise of influence. His fellow-plenipotentiaries were dummies; and even the trusted Colonel House, with vastly more knowledge of men and of Europe than the President, from whose sensitiveness the President's dullness had gained so much, fell into the background as time went on. All this was encouraged by his colleagues on the Council of Four, who, by the break-up of the Council of Ten, completed the isolation which the President's own temperament had initiated. Thus day after day and week after week he allowed himself to be closeted, unsupported, unadvised, and alone, with men much sharper than himself, in situations of supreme difficulty, where he needed for success every description of resource, fertility, and knowledge. He allowed himself to be drugged by their atmosphere, to discuss on the basis of their plans and of their data, and to be led along their paths.

These and other various causes combined to produce the following situation. The reader must remember that the processes which are here compressed into a few pages took place slowly, gradually, insidiously, over a period of about five months.

As the President had thought nothing out, the Council was generally working on the basis of a French or British draft. He had to take up, therefore, a persistent attitude of obstruction, criticism, and negation if the draft was to become at all in line with his own ideas and purpose. If he was met on some points with apparent generosity (for there was always a safe margin of quite preposterous suggestions which no one took seriously), it was difficult for him not to yield on others. Compromise was inevitable, and never to compromise on the essential very difficult. Besides, he was soon made to appear to be taking the German part, and laid himself open to the suggestion (to which he was foolishly and unfortunately sensitive) of being "pro-German."

After a display of much principle and dignity in the early days of the Council of Ten, he discovered that there were certain very important points in the programme of his French, British, or Italian colleague, as the case might be, of which he was incapable of securing the surrender by the methods of secret diplomacy. What then was he to do in the last resort? He could let the Conference drag on an endless length by the exercise of sheer obstinacy. He could break it up and return to America in a rage with nothing settled. Or he could attempt an appeal to the world over the heads of the Conference. These were wretched alternatives, against each of which a great deal could be said. They were also very risky—especially for a politician. The President's mistaken policy over the Congressional election had weakened his personal position in his own country, and it was by no means certain that the American public would support him in a position of intransigency. It would mean a campaign in which the issues would be clouded by every sort of personal and party consideration, and who could say if right would triumph in a struggle which would certainly not be decided on its merits. Besides, any open rupture with his colleagues would certainly bring upon his head the blind passions of "anti-German" resentment with which the public of all allied countries were still inspired. They would not listen to his arguments. They would not be cool enough to treat the issue as one of international morality or of the right governance of Europe. The cry would simply be that for various sinister and selfish reasons the President wished "to let the Hun off." The almost unanimous voice of the French and British Press could be anticipated. Thus, if he threw down the gage publicly he might be defeated. And if he were defeated, would not the final Peace be far worse than if he were to retain his prestige and endeavour to make it as good as the limiting conditions of European politics would allow him? But above all, if he were defeated, would he not lose the League of Nations? And was not this, after all, by far the most important issue for the future happiness of the world? The Treaty would be altered and softened by time. Much in it which now seemed so vital would become trifling, and much which was impracticable would for that very reason never happen.   But the League, even in an imperfect form, was permanent; it was the first commencement of a new principle in the government of the world; Truth and Justice in international relations could not be established in a few months—they must be born in due course by the slow gestation of the League.   Clemenceau had been clever enough to let it be seen that he would swallow the League at a price.

At the crisis of his fortunes the President was a lonely man.   Caught up in the toils of the Old World, he stood in great need of sympathy, of moral support, of the enthusiasm of masses. But buried in the Conference, stifled in the hot and poisoned atmosphere of Paris, no echo reached him from the outer world, and no throb of passion, sympathy, or encouragement from his silent constituents in all countries.   He felt that the blaze of popularity which had greeted his arrival in Europe was already dimmed; the Paris Press jeered at him openly; his political opponents at home were taking advantage of his absence to create an atmosphere against him; England was cold, critical, and unresponsive.   He had so formed his *entourage* that he did not receive through private channels the current of faith and enthusiasm of which the public sources seemed dammed up.   He needed, but lacked, the added strength of collective faith. The German terror still overhung us, and even the sympathetic public was very cautious; the enemy must not be encouraged, our friends must be supported, this was not the time for discord or agitations, the President must be trusted to do his best. And in this drought the flower of the President's faith withered and dried up.

Thus it came to pass that the President countermanded the *George Washington*, which, in a moment of well-founded rage, he had ordered to be in readiness to carry him from the treacherous halls of Paris back to the seat of his authority, where he could have felt himself again. But as soon, alas, as he had taken the road of compromise the defects, already indicated, of his temperament and of his equipment were fatally apparent. He could take the high line; he could practise obstinacy; he could write Notes from Sinai or Olympus; he could remain unapproachable in the White House or even in the Council of Ten and be safe. But if he once stepped down to the intimate equality of the Four, the game was evidently up.

Now it was that what I have called his theological or Presbyterian temperament became dangerous. Having decided that some concessions were unavoidable, he might have sought by firmness and address and the use of the financial power of the United States to secure as much as he could of the substance, even at some sacrifice of the letter. But the President was not capable of so clear an understanding with himself as this implied. He was too conscientious. Although compromises were now necessary, he remained a man of principle and the Fourteen Points a contract absolutely binding upon him. He would do nothing that was not honourable; he would do nothing that was not just and right; he would do nothing that was contrary to his great profession of faith. Thus, without any abatement of the verbal inspiration of the Fourteen Points, they became a document for gloss and interpretation and for all the intellectual apparatus of self-deception, by which, I dare say, the President's forefathers had persuaded themselves that the course they thought it necessary to take was consistent with every syllable of the Pentateuch.

The President's attitude to his colleagues had now become: I want to meet you so far as I can; I see your difficulties and I should like to be able to agree to what you propose, but I can do nothing that is not just and right, and you must first of all show me that what you want does really fall within the words of the pronouncements which are binding on me. Then began the weaving of that web of sophistry and

Jesuitical exegesis that was finally to clothe with
insincerity the language and substance of the
whole Treaty. The word was issued to the
witches of all Paris:

> Fair is foul, and foul is fair,
> Hover through the fog and filthy air.

The subtlest sophisters and most hypocritical
draftsmen were set to work, and produced many
ingenious exercises which might have deceived
for more than an hour a cleverer man than the
President.

Thus instead of saying that German Austria
is prohibited from uniting with Germany except
by leave of France (which would be inconsistent
with the principle of self-determination), the
Treaty, with delicate draftsmanship, states that
"Germany acknowledges and will respect strictly
the independence of Austria, within the frontiers
which may be fixed in a Treaty between that
State and the Principal Allied and Associated
Powers; she agrees that this independence shall
be inalienable, except with the consent of the
Council of the League of Nations," which
sounds, but is not, quite different. And
who knows but that the President forgot that
another part of the Treaty provides that for
this purpose the Council of the League must
be *unanimous*.

Instead of giving Danzig to Poland, the

Treaty establishes Danzig as a "Free" City, but includes this "Free" City within the Polish Customs frontier, entrusts to Poland the control of the river and railway system, and provides that "the Polish Government shall undertake the conduct of the foreign relations of the Free City of Danzig as well as the diplomatic protection of citizens of that city when abroad."

In placing the river system of Germany under foreign control, the Treaty speaks of declaring international those "river systems which naturally provide more than one State with access to the sea, with or without transhipment from one vessel to another."

Such instances could be multiplied. The honest and intelligible purpose of French policy, to limit the population of Germany and weaken her economic system, is clothed, for the President's sake, in the august language of freedom and international equality.

But perhaps the most decisive moment, in the disintegration of the President's moral position and the clouding of his mind, was when at last, to the dismay of his advisers, he allowed himself to be persuaded that the expenditure of the Allied Governments on pensions and separation allowances could be fairly regarded as "damage done to the civilian population of the Allied and Associated Powers by German aggression by land, by sea, and from the air," in a sense in which the other expenses of the war could not be so regarded. It was a long theological struggle in which, after the rejection of many different arguments, the President finally capitulated before a masterpiece of the sophist's art.[1]

At last the work was finished, and the President's conscience was still intact. In spite of everything, I believe that his temperament allowed him to leave Paris a really sincere man; and it is probable that to his death he was genuinely convinced that the Treaty contained practically nothing inconsistent with his former professions.

But the work was too complete, and to this was due the last tragic episode of the drama. The reply of Brockdorff-Rantzau naturally took the line that Germany had laid down her arms on the basis of certain assurances, and that the Treaty in many particulars was not consistent with these assurances. But this was exactly what the President could not admit; in the sweat of solitary contemplation and with prayers to God he had done *nothing* that was not just and right; for the President to admit that the German reply had force in it was to destroy his

[1] [For the details of this piece of work *vide* the author's *A Revision of the Treaty*, chap. v.]

self-respect and to disrupt the inner equipoise of his soul, and every instinct of his stubborn nature rose in self-protection. In the language of medical psychology, to suggest to the President that the Treaty was an abandonment of his professions was to touch on the raw a Freudian complex. It was a subject intolerable to discuss, and every subconscious instinct plotted to defeat its further exploration.

Thus it was that Clemenceau brought to success what had seemed to be, a few months before, the extraordinary and impossible proposal that the Germans should not be heard. If only the President had not been so conscientious, if only he had not concealed from himself what he had been doing, even at the last moment he was in a position to have recovered lost ground and to have achieved some very considerable successes. But the President was set. His arms and legs had been spliced by the surgeons to a certain posture, and they must be broken again before they could be altered. To his horror, Mr. Lloyd George, desiring at the last moment all the moderation he dared, discovered that he could not in five days persuade the President of error in what it had taken five months to prove to him to be just and right. After all, it was harder to de-bamboozle this old Presbyterian than it had been to bamboozle him, for the former involved his belief in and respect for himself.

Thus in the last act the President stood for stubbornness and a refusal of conciliations.

MR. LLOYD GEORGE

A Fragment

I wrote the preceding description of the Council of Four
in the summer of 1919 immediately after my resignation
as Treasury representative at the Peace Conference.
Friends, to whom I showed it for criticism, pressed me
to add a further passage concerning Mr. Lloyd George,
and in an attempt to satisfy them I wrote what here
follows. But I was not content with it, and I did not
print it in *The Economic Consequences of the Peace*, where
the chapter on "The Conference" appeared as it was
originally written with no addendum. I was also
influenced by a certain compunction. I had been very
close to Mr. Lloyd George at certain phases of the
Conference, and I felt at bottom that this, like almost
everything else that one could say about him, was only
partial. I did not like to print in the heat of the moment
what seemed to me, even in the heat of the moment, to
be incomplete.

I feel some compunction still. But nearly fourteen
years have passed by. These matters belong now
to history. It is easier to explain than it was then,
that this is an aspect, a thing seen but not the whole
picture and to offer it as a record of how one, who

saw the process at close quarters, sincerely felt at the time.

I should prefer to end this chapter here. But the reader may ask, What part in the result did the British Prime Minister play? What share had England in the final responsibility? The answer to the second question is not clear-cut. And as to the first, who shall paint the chameleon, who can tether a broomstick? The character of Lloyd George is not yet rendered, and I do not aspire to the task.

The selfish, or, if you like, the legitimate interests of England did not, as it happened, conflict with the Fourteen Points as vitally as did those of France. The destruction of the fleet, the expropriation of the marine, the surrender of the colonies, the suzerainty of Mesopotamia — there was not much here for the President to strain at, even in the light of his professions, especially as England, whose diplomatic moderation as always was not hampered by the logical intransigency of the French mind, was ready to concede in point of form whatever might be asked. England did not desire the German fleet for herself, and its destruction was a phase of Disarmament. The expropriation of the marine was a legitimate compensation, specifically provided for in the pre-Armistice conditions, for the lawless campaign of submarines which had been the express occasion of America's entering the war. Over the colonies and Mesopotamia England demanded no exclusive sovereignty, and they were covered by the Doctrine of Mandates under the League of Nations.

Thus when the British Delegation left for Paris there seemed no insuperable obstacles to an almost complete understanding between the British and the American negotiators. There were only two clouds on the horizon—the so-called Freedom of the Seas and the Prime Minister's election pledges on the Indemnity. The first, to the general surprise, was never raised by the President, a silence which, presumably, was the price he deemed it judicious to pay for British co-operation on other more vital issues; the second was more important.

The co-operation, which was thus rendered possible, was largely realised in practice. The individual members of the British and American delegations were united by bonds of fraternal feeling and mutual respect, and constantly worked together and stood together for a policy of honest dealing and broad-minded humanity. And the Prime Minister, too, soon established

D

himself as the President's friend and powerful ally against the Latins' alleged rapacity or lack of international idealism. Why then did not the joint forces of these two powerful and enlightened autocrats give us the Good Peace?

The answer is to be sought more in those intimate workings of the heart and character which make the tragedies and comedies of the domestic hearthrug than in the supposed ambitions of empires or philosophies of statesmen. The President, the Tiger, and the Welsh witch were shut up in a room together for six months and the Treaty was what came out. Yes, the Welsh *witch*—for the British Prime Minister contributed the female element to this triangular intrigue. I have called Mr. Wilson a nonconformist clergyman. Let the reader figure Mr. Lloyd George as a *femme fatale*. An old man of the world, a *femme fatale*, and a nonconformist clergyman—these are the characters of our drama. Even though the lady was very religious at times, the Fourteen Commandments could hardly expect to emerge perfectly intact.

I must try to silhouette the broomstick as it sped through the twilit air of Paris.

Mr. Lloyd George's devotion to duty at the Paris Conference was an example to all servants of the public. He took no relaxation, enjoyed no pleasures, had no life and no occupation

save that of Prime Minister and England's
spokesman.   His labours were immense and
he spent his vast stores of spirit and of energy
without stint on the formidable task he had
put his hand to.   His advocacy of the League
of Nations was sincere; his support of a fair
application of the principle of Self-Determination to Germany's eastern frontiers was disinterested.   He had no wish to impose a
Carthaginian Peace; the crushing of Germany
was no part of his purpose.   His hatred of war
is real, and the strain of pacifism and radical
idealism, which governed him during the Boer
War, is a genuine part of his composition.   He
would have defended a Good Peace before the
House of Commons with more heart than he
did that which he actually brought back to
them.

But in such a test of character and method
as Paris provided, the Prime Minister's naturally good instincts, his industry, his inex-
haustible nervous vitality were not serviceable.
In that furnace other qualities were called for—
a policy deeply grounded in permanent principle, tenacity, fierce indignation, honesty, loyal
leadership.   If Mr. Lloyd George had no good
qualities, no charms, no fascinations, he would
not be dangerous.   If he were not a syren, we
need not fear the whirlpools.

But it is not appropriate to apply to him the ordinary standards. How can I convey to the reader, who does not know him, any just impression of this extraordinary figure of our time, this syren, this goat-footed bard, this half-human visitor to our age from the hag-ridden magic and enchanted woods of Celtic antiquity? One catches in his company that flavour of final purposelessness, inner irresponsibility, existence outside or away from our Saxon good and evil, mixed with cunning, remorselessness, love of power, that lend fascination, enthralment, and terror to the fair-seeming magicians of North European folklore. Prince Wilson sailing out from the West in his barque *George Washington* sets foot in the enchanted castle of Paris to free from chains and oppression and an ancient curse the maid Europe, of eternal youth and beauty, his mother and his bride in one. There in the castle is the King with yellow parchment face, a million years old, and with him an enchantress with a harp singing the Prince's own words to a magical tune. If only the Prince could cast off the paralysis which creeps on him and, crying to heaven, could make the Sign of the Cross, with a sound of thunder and crashing glass the castle would dissolve, the magicians vanish, and Europe leap to his arms. But in this fairy-tale the forces of the half-

world win and the soul of Man is subordinated
to the spirits of the earth.

Lloyd George is rooted in nothing; he is
void and without content; he lives and feeds
on his immediate surroundings; he is an instrument and a player at the same time which plays
on the company and is played on by them too;
he is a prism, as I have heard him described,
which collects light and distorts it and is most
brilliant if the light comes from many quarters
at once; a vampire and a medium in one.

Whether by chance or by design, the principal
British war aims (with the exception of the Indemnity, if this was one of them) were dealt
with in the earliest stages of the Conference.
Clemenceau was criticised at the time for his
tardiness in securing the primary demands of
France. But events proved him to be right in
not forcing the pace. The French demands,
as I have pointed out, were much more controversial than those of the British; and it was
essential to get the British well embroiled in a
Peace of selfish interests before putting the
professions of the Conference to a severer
test. The British demands afforded an excellent *hors-d'œuvre* to accustom the delicate
palate of the President to the stronger flavours
which were to come. This order of procedure
laid the British Prime Minister open to the

charge, whenever he seemed too critical of
French demands, that, having first secured
every conceivable thing that he wanted himself,
he was now ready with characteristic treachery
to abandon his undertakings to his French
comrades. In the atmosphere of Paris this
seemed a much more potent taunt than it really
was. But it gained its real strength, in its
influence on the Prime Minister, from three
special attendant circumstances. In two respects
the Prime Minister found himself unavoidably
and inextricably on Clemenceau's side—in the
matters of the Indemnity and of the Secret
Treaties. If the President's morale was maintained intact, Mr. Lloyd George could not hope
to get his way on these issues; he was, therefore, almost equally interested with Clemenceau
in gradually breaking down this morale. But,
besides, he had Lord Northcliffe and the British
Jingoes on his heels, and complaints in the
French Press were certain to find their echo in
a certain section of the British also.

If, therefore, he were to take his stand firmly
and effectively on the side of the President,
there was needed an act of courage and faith
which could only be based on fundamental
beliefs and principles. But Mr. Lloyd George
has none such, and political considerations
pointed to a middle path.

Precisely, therefore, as the President had found himself pushed along the path of compromise, so also did the Prime Minister, though for very different reasons.   But while the President failed because he was very bad at the game of compromise, the Prime Minister trod the way of ill-doing because he was far too good at it.

The reader will thus apprehend how Mr. Lloyd George came to occupy an ostensibly middle position, and how it became his rôle to explain the President to Clemenceau and Clemenceau to the President and to seduce everybody all round.   He was only too well fitted for the task, but much better fitted for dealing with the President than with Clemenceau. Clemenceau was much too cynical, much too experienced, and much too well educated to be taken in, at his age, by the fascinations of the lady from Wales.   But for the President it was a wonderful, almost delightful, experience to be taken in hand by such an expert.   Mr. Lloyd George had soon established himself as the President's only real friend.   The President's very masculine characteristics fell a complete victim to the feminine enticements, sharpness, quickness, sympathy of the Prime Minister.

We have Mr. Lloyd George, therefore, in

his middle position, but exercising more sway over the President than over Clemenceau. Now let the reader's mind recur to the metaphors. Let him remember the Prime Minister's incurable love of a deal; his readiness to surrender the substance for the shadow; his intense desire, as the months dragged on, to get a conclusion and be back to England again. What wonder that in the eventual settlement the real victor was Clemenceau.

Even so, close observers never regarded it as impossible right up to the conclusion of the affair that the Prime Minister's better instincts and truer judgement might yet prevail — he knew in his heart that this Peace would disgrace him and that it might ruin Europe. But he had dug a pit for himself deeper than even he could leap out of; he was caught in his own toils, defeated by his own methods. Besides, it is a characteristic of his inner being, of his kinship with the trolls and the soulless simulacra of the earth, that at the great crises of his fortunes it is the lower instincts of the hour that conquer.

These were the personalities of Paris — I forbear to mention other nations or lesser men: Clemenceau, aesthetically the noblest; the President, morally the most admirable; Lloyd George, intellectually the subtlest. Out of their disparities and weaknesses the Treaty was born, child of the least worthy attributes of each of its parents, without nobility, without morality, without intellect.

MR. BONAR LAW

MR. BONAR LAW's breakdown[1] is a great misfortune, not less to his political opponents than to his own supporters. We shall not easily find another leader of the Conservative Party who is so *unprejudiced*. Mr. Bonar Law has been, before everything, a party man, deeply concerned for his party, obedient to its instincts, and at each crisis the nominee of its machine. On two crucial questions, Tariff Reform and the support of Ulster, he adopted with vehemence the extreme party view. Yet, in truth, he was almost devoid of Conservative principles. This Presbyterian from Canada has no imaginative reverence for the traditions and symbols of the past, no special care for vested interests, no attachment whatever to the Upper Classes, the City, the Army, or the Church. He is prepared to consider each question on its merits, and his candid acknowledgement of the case for a Capital Levy

This note was written during Bonar Law's lifetime, on the occasion of his final retirement from office.

42

was a striking example of an habitual state of mind.

Mr. Bonar Law's Conservatism was not based on dogma, or prejudice, or a passion to preserve certain sides of English life. It proceeded from caution, scepticism, lack of faith, a distrust of any intellectual process which proceeded more than one or two steps ahead, or any emotional enthusiasm which grasped at an intangible object, and an extreme respect for all kinds of *Success*.

Mr. Bonar Law's great skill in controversy, both in private conversation and in public debate, was due not only to the acuteness of his mind and his retentive memory which have impressed all observers, but also to his practice of limiting the argument to the pieces, so to speak, actually on the board and to the two or three moves ahead which could be definitely foreseen. (Mr. Bonar Law avowedly carried his well-known passion for the technique of chess into the problems of politics; and it is natural to use chess metaphors to describe the workings of his mind.) Mr. Bonar Law was difficult to answer in debate because he nearly always gave the perfectly sensible reply, on the assumption that the pieces visible on the board constituted the whole premises of the argument, that any attempt to look far ahead was too hypothetical and difficult to be worth while, and that one was playing the game in question *in vacuo*, with no ulterior purpose except to make the right move in that particular game. This method of his gained him perhaps more credit for candour and sincerity, as compared with other people, than he really deserved. He has been at times just as sly as other politicians; not, as he once pointed out, quite so simple as he looks. But it has been much easier for him to express, on any given occasion, more or less the whole contents of his mind, and very nearly his *real* reasons without reserve or ulterior purpose, than for others, some of whose reasons were too remote to be easily expressed or were not solely connected with the particular matter in hand, or could not be conveniently introduced on that occasion. An opponent who was trying to look some considerable way ahead, or saw the immediate position in the vague outlines of its relation to the situation as a whole, or had ultimate ideals which it would be priggish to mention too often, would always find himself at a great disadvantage in arguing with Mr. Bonar Law. His quietness and sweet reasonableness and patient attention to the more tangible parts of what his opponent had just said would bring into strong relief anything hysterical or overdone in the opposition attitude.

No mind, amongst those who waged war for this country, was swifter on the surface of things than his; there was no one who could be briefed quicker than he and put *au courant* with the facts of the case in those hurried moments which a Civil Servant gets with his chief before a Conference; and no one who could remember so much from a previous acquaintance with the question.   But this swiftness of apprehension, not only of facts and arguments but also of persons and their qualities, even in combination with his objective, chessplaying mind, did not save him from a quite decided anti-intellectualist bias.   Those who were present at Trinity Commem. some four years ago will remember a charming little speech given to the undergraduates after dinner, in which he dismissed with sweet-tempered cynicism everything a University stands for. Mr. Bonar Law has liked to think of himself as a plain business man, who could have made a lot of money if he had chosen to, with a good judgement of markets rather than of long-period trends, right on the short swing, handling wars and empires and revolutions with the coolness and limited purpose of a first-class captain of industry.   This distrust of intellectualist probings into unrealised possibilities leads him to combine great caution and pessim-

ism about the chances of the immediate situation with considerable recklessness about what
may happen eventually—a characteristic running through his policy both during and since
the war. He would hold, for example, that it
was an almost hopeless proposition to prevent
France from going into the Ruhr, but that the
consequences of her doing so, though very bad,
might not be quite so bad as some people
anticipate. This quality prevented him sometimes from being as good a negotiator as might
have been expected. He was not held back
from yielding a little too much either by cheerful
optimism about the prospects of pulling off a
better bargain or by getting frightened about
the remoter consequences of giving way. Perhaps, after all, he might not have made a very
successful business man — too pessimistic to
snatch present profits and too short-sighted to
avoid future catastrophe.

Mr. Bonar Law's inordinate respect for Success is noteworthy. He is capable of respecting
even an intellectualist who turns out right. He
admires self-made millionaires. He is not easily
shocked by the methods employed by others to
attain success. The great admiration in which
he formerly held Mr. Lloyd George was largely
based on the latter's success, and diminished
proportionately when the success fell off.

Modest, gentle, unselfish ways have won for him affection from all who have worked near him. But the feeling of the public is due, perhaps, to their instinctive apprehension of a larger, rarer thing about him than these simple qualities. They feel him to have been a great public servant, whose life of austerity and duty served them rather than himself. Many politicians are too much enthralled by the crash and glitter of the struggle, their hearts obviously warmed by the swell and pomp of authority, enjoying their positions and their careers, clinging to these sweet delights, and primarily pleasing themselves. These are the natural target of envy and detraction and a certain contempt. They have their reward already and need no gratitude. But the public have liked to see a Prime Minister not enjoying his lot unduly. We have preferred to be governed by the sad smile of one who adopts towards the greatest office in the State the attitude that whilst, of course, it is nice to be Prime Minister, it is no great thing to covet, and who feels in office, and not merely afterwards, the vanity of things.

May 1923.

LORD OXFORD

Those who only knew Lord Oxford in his later life must find it hard to credit either the appearance or the reputation which are reported to have been his thirty or more years ago. The ability and the reticence were there to be recognised, but the somewhat tight features, the alleged coldness of the aspiring lawyer from Balliol, were entirely transformed in the noble Roman of the war and post-war years, who looked the part of Prime Minister as no one has since Mr. Gladstone. His massive countenance and aspect of venerable strength were, in these later days, easily perceived to mask neither coldness nor egoism, but to clothe with an appropriate form a warm and tender heart easily touched to emotion, and a personal reserve which did not ask or claim anything for himself.

Lord Oxford possessed most of the needed gifts of a great statesman except ruthlessness towards others and insensitiveness for himself. One wonders whether in the conditions of the modern age a man so sensitive as he was will ever again be robust enough to expose himself to the outrages of public life. Lord Oxford protected his sensitiveness by silence, by totally refraining from retort or from complaint. He absolutely rejected the aid or the opportunities of the venal Press. He could be the leader of a Nation or of a Party; he would hasten to protect a friend or a colleague; but he disdained to protect himself to a degree which was scarcely compatible with the actual conditions of contemporary life. Yet it was probably this course of behaviour, this element of character, which, increasingly with years, moulded for him the aspect of dignity, the air of sweetness and calm, the gentle ruggedness of countenance, which those who knew him after he had finally left office will carry in their memories as characteristically his. He had, besides, a keen sense of the pleasure of simple things, and it was this capacity, perhaps, which helped him to face political disappointments, when they came, without self-pity.

It is natural to dwell at this moment on the qualities which made him lovable and were also those which events brought most to notice in the closing phase of his career—the phase after he had ceased to be Prime Minister, the last twelve years, which have contributed little or

E

nothing to his constructive services to the State, yet have greatly added to the world's knowledge and appreciation of his own personality. But it was, of course, his powers of intellect and of rapid industry which carried him to great offices of State. Lord Oxford's intellect combined rapidity of apprehension, lucidity, critical sharpness, a copious and accurate memory, taste and discrimination, freedom both from prejudices and from illusion, with an absence of originality and creative power; and I am not sure that this want of originality was not one of the most necessary of the ingredients to produce the successful combination. His mind was built for the purpose of dealing with the given facts of the outside world; it was a mill or a machine, not a mine or a springing field. But this deficiency conserved the strength of his judgement. Lord Oxford had no intellectual fancies to lead him astray, no balloons of his own making to lift his feet off the ground. It was his business to hear and to judge; and the positions he occupied—Home Secretary, Chancellor of the Exchequer, Prime Minister—are positions best occupied, not by one ingenious to invent and to build, but by one whose business it is to hear and to judge. For this business there has been no man in this century by any means his equal. Few words and little time were necessary for him to apprehend perfectly the purport of what he was being told; and he would bring his knowledge and experience to bear on it with an entire freedom from bias and *parti pris.*

His temperament was naturally conservative. With a little stupidity and a few prejudices dashed in he would have been Conservative in the political sense also. As it was, he was the perfect Whig for carrying into execution those Radical projects of his generation which were well judged. It is remarkable, looking back on the Liberal legislation of the eight years before the war, to see how abundant it was, yet how well chosen, and how completely on the whole it has stood the test of events. To Lord Oxford we owe, not the invention of any part of that programme, but the wisdom of its selection and execution. In the controversy as to the conduct of the war, which culminated in the downfall of the first Coalition Government at the end of 1916, I believed then, and I believe now, that he was largely in the right.

Few men can have accomplished in their lives more hard work than Lord Oxford. But he worked, as a Prime Minister must if he is to survive, with great economy of effort. He could deal with printed and written matter with the rapidity of a scholar. He never succumbed to the modern curse of shorthand and the verbosity it breeds. Lord Oxford belonged to the lineage of great men, which will, I pray, never die out, who can take up a pen and do what is necessary in short notes written in their own hand. Lord Oxford's fault, in relation to his work, lay, perhaps, in his willingness to relax his attention from it when it was put by, not to carry it about with him in his mind and on his tongue when the official day's work was done. Certainly this was a source of strength sometimes, but also, on occasion, of weakness. In combination with his reserve, which made it difficult to broach with him an awkward topic— in part the necessary equipment of any leading statesman to keep the impertinent at bay, but practised by him in an unusual degree—it would sometimes cut him off from full knowledge of what was brewing in the political cauldron. These habits of mind were also capable of facilitating an evasion, especially of a personal issue. The discipline and the harsh severity towards faithful friends and less faithful rivals alike which the management of a Cabinet must needs entail were to him extraordinarily distasteful.

Lord Oxford was, therefore, at his best and at his happiest when there were great issues afoot which were entirely political and not at all personal; when he had behind him a body of supporters and lieutenants united at heart and in intention, and only differing in the degrees of their impulsiveness. On such occasions he would be able to use, and direct into the courses of wisdom, all that is most valuable in a great political party. The fight for Free Trade, the fight for the Parliament Act, the opening year of the War were opportunities of this kind, when Mr. Asquith could stand up as a leader with the full powers of his intellect and composure of spirit.

It is to be recorded of Lord Oxford that he loved learning and studious ways and the things which a University stands for. He was a real reader; he could handle books in a library with love. The classical and literary pursuits, his aptitude for which had gained him his first step on the ladder, were not discarded when they had ceased to be useful. I think that he liked these things, just as he liked great constitutional and political controversies, all the better because they were not too much mixed with the soiled clay of personal issues.

Those who knew Lord Oxford intimately cannot think of him except in the environment of a unique family. He was the solid core round which that brilliant circle revolved—the centre of the gayest and brightest world, the widest-flung yet the simplest hospitality of modern England. With an incomparable hostess opposite him, with wit and abundance, indiscretion and all that was most rash and bold flying round him, Lord Oxford would love to appear the dullest amidst so much light, to rest himself, and to enjoy the flow of reason and of unreason, stroking his chin, shrugging his shoulders, a wise and tolerant umpire.

February 1928.

EDWIN MONTAGU

MOST of the newspaper accounts which I have read do less than justice to the remarkable personality of Edwin Montagu. He was one of those who suffer violent fluctuations of mood, quickly passing from reckless courage and self-assertion to abject panic and dejection—always dramatising life and his part in it, and seeing himself and his own instincts either in the most favourable or in the most unfavourable light, but seldom with a calm and steady view. Thus it was easy for the spiteful to convict him out of his own mouth, and to belittle his name by remembering him only when his face was turned towards the earth. At one moment he would be Emperor of the East riding upon an elephant, clothed in rhetoric and glory, but at the next a beggar in the dust of the road, crying for alms but murmuring under his breath cynical and outrageous wit which pricked into dustier dust the rhetoric and the glory.

That he was an Oriental, equipped, neverthe-

less, with the intellectual technique and atmosphere of the West, drew him naturally to the
political problems of India, and allowed an
instinctive, mutual sympathy between him and
its peoples. But he was interested in all political
problems and not least in the personal side of
politics, and was most intensely a politician.
Almost everything else bored him. Some
memoir-writers have suggested that he was
really a scientist, because with Nature he could
sometimes find escape from the footlights.
Others, judging from his parentage and from
his entering the City in the last two years of his
life, make out that he was, naturally, a financier.
This also is far from the truth. I saw him
intimately in the Treasury and in the financial
negotiations of the Peace Conference, and,
whilst his general judgement was good, I do not
think that he cared, or had great aptitude, for
the problems of pure finance. Nor—though
he loved money for what it could buy—was he
interested in the details of money-making.

Mr. Lloyd George was, of course, the un-
doing of his political career—as, indeed,
Montagu always said that he would be. He
could not keep away from that bright candle.
But he knew, poor moth, that he would burn
his wings. It was from his tongue that I, and
many others, have heard the most brilliant, true,

and witty descriptions of that (in his prime) undescribable. But whilst, behind the scenes, Montagu's tongue was master, his weaknesses made him, in action, the natural tool and victim; for, of all men, he was one of the easiest to use and throw on one side. It used to be alleged that a certain very Noble Lord had two footmen, of whom one was lame and the other swift of foot, so that letters of resignation carried by the one could be intercepted by the other before their fatal delivery at No. 10. Edwin Montagu's letters were not intercepted; but the subtle intelligencer of human weakness, who opened them, knew that by then the hot fit was over and the cold was blowing strong. They could be ignored or used against the writer—at choice.

I never knew a male person of big mind like his who was more addicted to gossip than Edwin Montagu. Perhaps this was the chief reason why he could not bear to be out of things. He was an inveterate gossip in the servants' hall of secretaries and officials. It was his delight to debate, at the Cabinet, affairs of State, and then to come out and deliver, to a little group, a brilliant and exposing parody, aided by mimicry, of what each of the great ones, himself included, had said. But he loved it better when he could push gossip over into intimacy.

He never went for long without an intense desire to unbosom himself, even to exhibit himself, and to squeeze out of his confidant a drop of—perhaps reluctant—affection. And then again he would be silent and reserved beyond bearing, sitting stonily with his great hand across his mouth and a staring monocle.

November 1924.

WINSTON CHURCHILL

Mr. Churchill on the War

This brilliant book[1] is not a history. It is a series of episodes, a succession of bird's-eye views, designed to illuminate certain facets of the great contest and to confirm the author's thesis about the conduct, in its broadest strategic aspects, of modern warfare. There are great advantages in this procedure. Mr. Churchill tells us many details of extraordinary interest, which most of us did not know before, but he does not lose himself in detail. He deals in the big with the essential problems of the higher thought of the conduct of the war. The book is written, like most books of any value, with a purpose. It does not pretend to the empty impartiality of those dull writers before whose minds the greatest and most stirring events of history can pass without producing any distinct impression one way or the other. Mr.

[1] *The World Crisis, 1916–1918.*

Churchill's was, perhaps, the most acute and concentrated intelligence which saw the war at close quarters from beginning to end with knowledge of the inside facts and of the inner thoughts of the prime movers of events. He formed clear conclusions as to where lay truth and error—not only in the light of after-events. And he here tells them to us in rhetorical, but not too rhetorical, language. This naturally means telling us most where he was nearest, and criticising chiefly where he deemed himself the wisest. But he contrives to do this without undue egotism. He pursues no vendettas, discloses no malice. Even the admirals and generals, who are the victims of his analysis, are not pursued too far. Mr. Asquith, Mr. Lloyd George, Mr. Balfour, Mr. Bonar Law, Sir Edward Carson—he speaks them all fair and friendly in recognition of their several qualities, not striking down those who did service because they have joints in their armour. Mr. Churchill writes better than any politician since Disraeli. The book, whether its bias is right or wrong, will increase his reputation.

Mr. Churchill's principal thesis amounts to the contention that, broadly speaking, in each country the professional soldiers, the "brass-hats," were, on the great questions of military policy, generally wrong—wrong on the weight of the argument beforehand and wrong on the weight of the evidence afterwards—whilst the professional politicians, the "frocks," as Sir Henry Wilson called them (a bit of a "frock" himself), were generally right. This is a question upon which at the time it was impossible for an outside observer to form a judgement, since, whilst it appeared to be the case that both sides committed cardinal errors at each turning-point of the war, no one could divide the responsibility between the Cabinets and the General Staffs. In England, popular opinion rallied on the whole to the generals— more picturesque, much more glorious figures than our old knock-about friends the "frocks," and enjoying the enormous advantage of never having to explain themselves in public. Mr. Churchill sets himself to redress this balance, to convince us, in the light of the full disclosures now available from every side, that wisdom lay on the whole with Asquith, Lloyd George, and himself, with Briand, Painlevé, and Clemenceau, with Bethmann-Hollweg and even the Crown Prince, and that it was Haig and Robertson, Joffre and Nivelle, Falkenhayn and Ludendorff who jeopardised or lost the war.

Let me try to summarise Mr. Churchill's indictment of the General Staffs. Each side signally lacked a Cunctator Maximus. No

Fabius arose to wait, to withdraw, to entice. The "brass-hats" were always in a hurry, hurrying to disclose their possession of new weapons of offence—the German poison-gas, the German U-boats, the British tanks—before they had accumulated enough of them to produce a decisive effect; hurrying to the useless slaughter of their dreadful "pushes." The strategic surrender, the deliberate withdrawal, the attempt to lure the enemy into a pocket where he could be taken in flank, all such expedients of the higher imagination of warfare, were scarcely attempted. Mangin's counter-stroke under the direction of Foch in July 1918, which both the French and British Staffs were inclined to deprecate and distrust, was one of the few such efforts. The ideas of the Staffs were from beginning to end elementary in the extreme—in attack, to find out the enemy in his strongest place and hurl yourself on him; in defence, to die heroically in the first ditch. There were only two important exceptions to this rule—the withdrawal of the Germans to the Hindenburg line in 1917, and the unchanging demeanour of Sir John Jellicoe. Mr. Churchill's fascinating analysis of the Battle of Jutland seems to the layman to show that Jellicoe missed his chances —chances which he ought to have taken. But Jellicoe, carrying a greater burden of risk and responsibility than any other single individual, the only man on either side, as Mr. Churchill admits, who could have lost the war in an afternoon, does stand out as the one triumphant Cunctator who, though he may have missed chances, carried through from start to finish without a single disastrous mistake. I do not think, even in the light of some incisive criticisms which Mr. Churchill is able to make, that one would have wished to see any other personality, which the war threw up in any country, in charge of the North Sea.

Mr. Churchill's next point concerns the narrow geographical vision of the General Staffs, their inability on both sides to throw out wide-ranging glances of strategic and political imagination over the whole potential field of hostilities. The armies were drawn to one another like magnets. The soldiers were always busy discerning where the enemy was strongest and then demanding equal or greater forces to counter him, never testing where he was weakest and thrusting there. This is an old controversy upon which we have long known where Mr. Churchill stood, and Mr. Lloyd George also. I do not know that this book adds much directly to their case, but Mr. Churchill's third point, which I come to later, does confirm, I think, the potential value of the

restless visions of the politicians as hints towards victory, as against the dogged dullness of
the Staffs. Mr. Churchill holds that the
Germans, especially Falkenhayn, were at least
as much at fault in this respect as we were. The
Generals on both sides were equally confirmed
"Westerners," and supported one another, by
their dispositions, against their respective Governments at home.

Akin to this narrow geographical and political
outlook was the narrow scientific vision of the
professional soldiers, their extraordinary slowness to take up with new mechanical ideas, as
illustrated by the history of the tanks, which our
Staff deprecated in their inception and never
demanded from the Ministry of Munitions in
adequate quantity, even after they had become
enthusiastic of their results, and which Ludendorff never imitated on a serious scale, even
after their existence had been prematurely discovered to him. The overdoing of the artillery
and the maintenance of cavalry, which even in
1918 occupied nearly the same numbers of
British personnel as the machine guns and nearly
twice those of the tanks, are further examples
of inelasticity of mind, as compared with the
alternative policy, never adopted, except by Mr.
Churchill himself in 1918 with a view to the
unfought campaign of 1919, of an immense

concentration of man-power on aeroplanes, machine guns, tanks, and gas.

The third point, which probably constitutes the most novel and interesting part of Mr. Churchill's book, concerns the actual value, as judged by the results now fully known from the records of both sides, of the great offensives on the Western Front. It is here that there was the sharpest and most continuing divergence of opinion between the professional politicians and the professional soldiers. Apart from a temporary conversion of Mr. Lloyd George to the Staff view in 1917, the former were ever of the opinion that the soldiers were underestimating the opportunities of defence and overestimating the potential gains of an offensive, and that no decision would ever be reached by assaulting the enemy in his fortified positions on the Western Front. The influence of the War Cabinet was almost invariably cast against the "pushes" of 1915, 1916, and 1917. Since the successive Cabinets expected little from these appalling offensives, there was nothing to mitigate the effect on their minds of the cruel and useless losses. By the end of 1917 a situation was actually reached in which Mr. Lloyd George was preventing available troops from being sent across the Channel which were certainly required in reserve there, because he

F

could not trust his power to prevent Sir Douglas Haig from sending them to the massacre once they were in France. "But for the horror which Paschandaele inspired in the minds of the Prime Minister and the War Cabinet," Mr. Churchill writes, "Haig would no doubt have been supplied with very much larger reinforcements." Beginning with Mr. Asquith's prolonged and tenacious opposition to conscription down to this episode in the winter of 1917, Mr. Churchill's evidence goes to show that it was the politicians who had the soft hearts, but also that it was they on the whole who, on military grounds, were right.

The General Staffs were ready to admit after each offensive that the results were disappointing, but they were apt to console themselves with the consideration of the great losses inflicted on the enemy and on some satisfactory progress towards the objective of attrition. Mr. Churchill claims that he distrusted these conclusions at the time, and that the figures of casualties now available from both sides show that the result of almost every offensive was to leave the attacking side relatively weaker in man-power than it was before. Sir Frederick Maurice, in a letter to *The Times*, has disputed this interpretation of the statistics. But even if Mr. Churchill has pushed his case too far, he

seems on the whole to have established it.   In
particular it was Ludendorff's apparently successful offensive of 1918 which really prepared
the way for, and indeed rendered inevitable, the
final German collapse.

Nothing is more interesting in Mr. Churchill's
book than his impressions of the prevailing types
of the High Command on each side.   "There
was altogether lacking," he says, "that supreme
combination of the King-Warrior-Statesman
which is apparent in the persons of the great
conquerors of history."   Most of the great
Commanders, with the possible exception of
Joffre, were undoubtedly men of outstanding
ability in their profession, but they were pre-
vailingly of the heavy block-head type, men
whose nerves were much stronger than their
imaginations.   Hindenburg was not the only
wooden image.   Joffre, Kitchener, Haig,
Robertson, Ludendorff—they also might be
commemorated in the same medium.   They
slept well, they ate well—*nothing* could upset
them.   As they could seldom explain themselves and preferred to depend on their "instincts," they could never be refuted.   Mr.
Churchill, quoting from a letter from Robertson
to Haig in which the former proposes to stick to
offensives in the West "more because my instinct prompts me to stick to it, than because of

any good argument by which I can support it,"
comments: "These are terrible words when
used to sustain the sacrifice of nearly four
hundred thousand men." The type reached
its furthest limit in Mr. Churchill's semi-comic
portrait of Père Joffre. No doubt more highly
strung men could not stand the wear and tear of
High Command in modern warfare. They
were necessarily eliminated in favour of those
who, in Mr. Churchill's words, could preserve
their sang-froid amid disastrous surprises "to
an extent almost indistinguishable from insen-
sibility." Moreover, the Commander-in-Chief
may be almost the last person even to hear the
truth. "The whole habit of mind of a military
staff is based upon subordination of opinion."
This meant that the lighter mind of the politician,
surrounded by candid friends and watchful
opponents, was indispensable to the right conclusions. The final defeat of Germany was in
fact due to the supreme strength of her Great
General Staff. If Germany's politicians had
had the same influence as ours or France's or
America's she could never have suffered a
similar defeat. Her three cardinal errors,
according to Mr. Churchill—the invasion of
Belgium, the unrestricted use of U-boats, the
offensive of March 1918—were all the peculiar
and exclusive responsibility of the General Staff.

Ludendorff was the final embodiment both of the influence of the General Staff and of its highest qualities—of that General Staff whose members

were bound together by the closest ties of professional comradeship and common doctrine. They were to the rest of the Army what the Jesuits in their greatest period had been to the Church of Rome. Their representatives at the side of every Commander and at Headquarters spoke a language and preserved confidences of their own. The German Generals of Corps and Armies, Army-Group Commanders, nay, Hindenburg himself, were treated by this confraternity, to an extent almost incredible, as figureheads, and frequently as nothing more.

It was this extraordinary confraternity which raised the German military might to monstrous dimensions, provoked and organised inhuman exertions, and yet, by the inevitable workings of its own essence, brought down upon itself the great defeat.

Mr. Churchill does not dissemble his own delight in the intense experiences of conducting warfare on the grand scale which those can enjoy who make the decisions. Nor, on the other hand, does he conceal its awfulness for those who provide the raw material of those delights. The bias of emphasis is on the grand decisions and high arguments. But, not the less for this reason, is his book, in its final impression on the reader, a tractate against war—more effective than the work of a pacifist could be, a demonstration from one who loves the game, not only of the imbecility of its aims and of its methods, but, more than this, that the imbecility is not an accidental quality of the particular players, but is inherent in its spirit and its rules.

March 1927.

MR. CHURCHILL ON THE PEACE

MR. CHURCHILL has finished his task—by far and away the greatest contribution to the history of the war, the only one which combines the gifts of the historian and born writer with the profound experiences and direct knowledge of one of the prime movers of events. This last volume[1] is not so good, I think, as the two which preceded it—a falling away which is probably one more of the disappointing consequences of the author's latest bout of office. For authorship is a whole-time job; and so is the Chancellorship of the Exchequer. But it is much better than those who have read the rather flat, rhetorical extracts published by *The Times* will

[1] *The World Crisis : the Aftermath.*

have surmised.   For these lose, as extracts do,
the sweep and impression of the whole.

Mr. Churchill records in his preface what a
number of important events in which he was
personally concerned had utterly passed from
his mind.   This, he adds, is probably an experience common to most of the principal actors
—"one impression effaced another."   So with
anyone who lived in the administrative flux.
For me the quality of the Midland Railway
breakfast marmalade served up in the Hotel
Majestic has stuck faster than anything else; I
know *exactly* what that experience was like.   It
is only for those who lived for months in the
trenches or suffered some repetitive military
routine, where one impression reinforced another, that the war can in memory be lived
over again.   Yet Mr. Churchill has contrived
to convey a contemporary impression of motives
and atmosphere—though, curiously, least of all
by the contemporary documents he quotes,
which the reader will instinctively skip—such
as posterity would never be able to reconstruct
for itself.   The book contains, too, some
singularly moving passages, where the emotions
of the moment had left behind them a permanent furrow, of which I would particularly
instance the accounts of the British Demobilisa-
tion and of the Irish Treaty.   Moreover, it

serves to bring back to us with overwhelming
effect what of everything we are most disposed
to forget—the violence, bloodshed, and tumult
of the *post*-war years, the "Aftermath" of Mr.
Churchill's title.

The book is mainly made up of four distinct
topics, of which the successive chapters are,
rather distractingly, intermixed—the Peace
Conference, the Russian Revolution, the Irish
Rebellion, and the Greco-Turkish Imbroglio.
Of these the account of the Russian business is
—as one might expect—the least satisfactory.
Mr. Churchill does not seek to defend unduly
his own part in the fiascos of the Russian Civil
Wars. But he fails to see—or at least to set—in
perspective the bigness of the events in their
due relations, or to disentangle the essential
from casual episodes. He half admits the inevitable futility of the proceedings which he
supported; he lets one see the wretched character and effete incompetence of the Russian
Whites whom he would have so much liked to
idealise ("It was not the want of material means,
but of comradeship, will-power, and rugged
steadfastness that lost the struggle"); and he
quotes Foch, who firmly refused to have anything to do with the affair, as remarking "with
much discernment" that "these armies of
Koltchak and Denikin cannot last long because

they have no civil Governments behind them."
But the Bolsheviks remain for him, in spite of
his tribute to the greatness of Lenin, nothing
more than an imbecile atrocity.　His imagination cannot see them as the Great Scavengers,
and the officers of the Whites as better employed
on the films.　Yet can he believe that his fine
peroration——"Russia, self-outcast, sharpens her
bayonets in her Arctic night, and mechanically
proclaims through self-starved lips her philosophy of hatred and death"——is really the whole
of the truth?

Apart from Russia, Mr. Churchill appears, in
a degree to which public opinion has done much
less than justice, as an ardent and persistent
advocate of the policy of appeasement——appeasement in Germany, in Ireland, in Turkey.　As
he wrote to Mr. Lloyd George in March 1920
——"Since the Armistice my policy would have
been, 'Peace with the German people, war on
the Bolshevik tyranny.'"　Throughout the
Peace Conference such influence as he had was
cast on the side of moderation.

His account of the Peace Conference itself is
less personal in character than any other part of
the book, for he was, indeed, but little directly
concerned with it.　He visited Paris once or
twice, but was mainly in London preoccupied
with other matters.　It is, therefore, a general

view which he presents, as it appeared to a member of the British Cabinet who was outside the main stream of the negotiations. His attitude is to deplore — but to shrug his shoulders. There has been too much shrugging of the shoulders both at the time and since. He justifies his shrug on two grounds: firstly, because politicians are not only pusillanimous, but rightly so, their pusillanimity being merely a realisation of their actual impotence; and, secondly, because financial and economic mistakes work themselves out in due course, whereas frontiers, which were not so badly handled by the Conference, are the only long-period realities. One could say the same thing about the miseries of the war itself—they are all over now—and indeed about most things, for the consequences, even if they persist, are generally lost in the river of time; and the doctrine that statesmen must always act contrary to their convictions, when to do otherwise would lose them office, implies that they are less easily replaceable than is really the case. I believed then, and I believe now, that it was a situation where an investment in political courage would have been marvellously repaid in the end.

Mr. Churchill's account of the Conference lacks the intensity of feeling which would be natural to one who had been tormented on the

spot. But it is, all the same, the best short
handbook yet written to the general character
of what really happened. There are one or two
points in it worth picking out. Mr. Churchill
does well to emphasise the prolongation of the
blockade of Germany through the first half of
1919 as a question of first-rate importance. The
remarkable history of the successive negotiations for the renewal of the Armistice and the
provisioning of Germany has never yet been
printed.[1] He recognises their importance, but
his account of them (pages 66, 67) is by no
means accurate, and indicates that he was not
conversant with, or has forgotten, the details.
It was not the "officials" who were to blame.
If any individual is to be picked out as chiefly
responsible for prolonging the dreadful priva-
tions of Central Europe, it must certainly be
the celebrated Monsieur Klotz. I think he is
right in saying that Mr. Lloyd George was quite
genuine about hanging the Kaiser and continued to harbour such sentiments long after
others had cooled off; but that he never, at any
time, entertained an illusion about Reparations
or made any statement which did not, if read
carefully, include a saving clause.

It is well, too, that he gives the world a fuller

[1] [I recorded my impressions of this episode soon after the
event, but the time to consign them to print is not yet.]

account than has been published before of the meeting of the British Empire Delegation convened by Mr. Lloyd George in Paris on June 1, 1919, to consider the German reply to the draft Treaty of Peace. The Prime Minister had called this meeting "to strengthen himself in his efforts to obtain a mitigation of the peace terms." Mr. Churchill himself circulated a memorandum, endorsed by the Chief of the Imperial General Staff, urging that we should, at least, meet the Germans half-way. These views were accepted by practically the whole of the Delegation and of the Cabinet, including Mr. Austen Chamberlain, who was then Chancellor of the Exchequer, Lord Birkenhead, Lord Milner, and Mr. Balfour. The meeting resolved that many important concessions should be made, and added a rider authorising the Prime Minister "to use the full weight of the entire British Empire even to the point of refusing the services of the British Army to advance into Germany, or the services of the British Navy to enforce the blockade of Germany." This was the second time that Mr. Lloyd George had made a genuine, but abortive, effort for a "good" Peace. But it was not to be. The plebiscite for Upper Silesia was obtained as an almost solitary concession. For the rest, it was President Wilson—as I have described in *The*

Economic Consequences of the Peace[1]—who at this stage was "not taking any."

Mr. Churchill has a good deal to say about President Wilson.   He has had the advantage not only of his own memories, but of Colonel House's latest volumes, which have cast on the scene so bright a side-light.   As the evidence accumulates, the impression is confirmed of a blind man, unbelievably out of touch with the realities of things, filled with all the wrong suspicions.   But peace to his spirit.   Mr. Churchill's summing up is just:

The influence of mighty, detached, and well-meaning America upon the European settlement was a precious agency of hope.   It was largely squandered in sterile conflicts and half-instructed and half-pursued interferences.   If President Wilson had set himself from the beginning to make common cause with Lloyd George and Clemenceau, the whole force of these three great men, the heads of the dominant nations, might have played with plenary and beneficent power over the wide scene of European tragedy.   He consumed his own strength and theirs in conflict in which he was always worsted.   He gained as an antagonist and corrector results which were pitifully poor compared to those which would have rewarded comradeship.   He might have made everything swift and easy.   He made everything slower and more difficult.   He might have carried a settlement at the time when leadership was

[1] [See pp. 28-30 above.]

strong. He acquiesced in second-rate solutions when the phase of exhaustion and dispersion had supervened. However, as Captain he went down with his ship.

The chronicle is finished. With what feelings does one lay down Mr. Churchill's two-thousandth page? Gratitude to one who can write with so much eloquence and feeling of things which are part of the lives of all of us of the war generation, but which he saw and knew much closer and clearer. Admiration for his energies of mind and his intense absorption of intellectual interest and elemental emotion in what is for the moment the matter in hand— which is his best quality. A little envy, perhaps, for his undoubting conviction that frontiers, races, patriotisms, even wars if need be, are ultimate verities for mankind, which lends for him a kind of dignity and even nobility to events, which for others are only a nightmare interlude, something to be permanently avoided.

March 1929.

THE GREAT VILLIERS
CONNECTION

Mr. Gun[1] has set himself to carry forward the fascinating subject which Galton invented—the collection of hereditary titbits connecting the famous and the moderately famous—quite a different subject from the scientific compilation of complete family trees of definitely determinable characteristics such as blue eyes, round heads, six toes, and the like. His method, like Galton's, is to take in turn each of a number of distinguished "connections" and to exhibit to us what a surprising number of celebrities are some sort of a cousin to one another.

One of the most striking of Mr. Gun's connections is by no means a novel one, yet not too hackneyed to be worth repeating—the cousinship of Dryden, Swift, and Horace Walpole. All three were descended from John Dryden of Canons Ashby, Northamptonshire, Dean Swift being a second cousin once removed, and

[1] W. T. J. Gun, *Studies in Hereditary Ability.*

Horace Walpole a first cousin three times removed of John Dryden the poet (Horace being
descended on his mother's side—and therefore
irrespective of doubts as to his paternity—from
Dryden's aunt Elizabeth). Mr. Gun is disposed to trace this magnificent display to the
wife of the original John Dryden—Elizabeth
Cope, daughter of Erasmus's friend and great-
granddaughter of Sir Ralph Verney, which
brings a good many others into the same connection, including Robert Harley. A representative to-day of this great Verney connection
is Lady Ottoline Morrell. If, on the other
hand, we remember that Lady Ottoline is not
only descended from Verney the mercer, but
also from Sir William Pierrepont (and through
his wife from Henry VII.'s Empson son of
Empson the sieve-maker), we establish her
cousinship with Francis Beaumont, Lord
Chesterfield, and Lady Mary Wortley Montagu. Our families themselves lose track of
their own ramifications; we wonder if Lady
Ottoline herself knows that she can call cousin
Beaumont, Dryden, Swift, Walpole, Harley,
and Chesterfield. Birds of a feather? Perhaps
one can perceive in the consanguinity a certain
persistent element.

Mr. Gun's analysis of the descendants of
John Reid, who fell at Flodden Field in 1515,

is more novel, at least to the present writer. Here there is a remarkable versatility—and perhaps also a common quality? In the eighteenth century Mr. John Reid was responsible for Boswell, Robertson the historian, Robert Adam the architect, and Brougham. Amongst his living descendants are Mr. Bertrand Russell, Mr. Harold Nicolson, Mr. Bruce Lockhart, and General Booth-Tucker of the Salvation Army. More birds of a feather?

Mr. Gun is at pains to show how many of the well-known writers of to-day have old blood in their veins. He reminds us that Prof. G. M. and Mr. R. C. Trevelyan and Miss Rose Macaulay are descendants of the Highlander Aulay Macaulay (and therefore near connections of T. B. Macaulay), of whose son Kenneth's book Dr. Johnson said: "Very well written except some foppery about liberty and slavery"; that Mr. Hugh Walpole, Mr. Lytton Strachey, Mr. Compton Mackenzie, Mr. Maurice Baring, and (he should surely have added) Mrs. Virginia Woolf can claim distinction for several generations; and that Mr. Aldous Huxley is not only the grandson of his grandfather, but the nephew of Mrs. Humphry Ward, who was the niece of Matthew Arnold.

There remains for mention the most remarkable family of all—the great Villiers connection

G

from whom are descended all the ambitious fascinators, with so much charm of countenance and voice and so hard a little nut somewhere inside, who were the favourites and mistresses of our monarchs in the seventeenth century and of the parliamentary democracy ever since. There cannot have been a Cabinet for two hundred years—save, perhaps, the two Labour Cabinets—which did not contain descendants of Sir George Villiers and Sir John St. John, two country gentlemen in the reign of James I., of whom the son of the former married the daughter of the latter. The famous progeny of these two families is far too extensive to follow out here in detail. But a simple list is impressive—the first Duke of Buckingham, favourite of James I.; Barbara, Countess of Castlemaine and Duchess of Cleveland, mistress of Charles II.; Arabella Churchill, mistress of James II.; Elizabeth, Countess of Orkney, mistress of William III. (whom Swift called "the wisest woman he had ever known"); the second Duke of Buckingham; Lord Rochester; Lord Sandwich; the Duke of Berwick; the Duke of Marlborough; the third Duke of Grafton (George III.'s Premier); the two Pitts; Charles James Fox; Charles Townshend; Lord Castlereagh; the Napiers; the Herveys; the Seymours, Marquises of Hertford; the Butes; the Jerseys; the Lansdownes;

the Cavendishes, Dukes of Devonshire; Lady
Hester Stanhope; Lady Mary Wortley Montagu; Fielding, and, amongst many living contemporaries of the same blood, Mr. Winston
Churchill and Viscount Grey of Fallodon. This
is, indeed, the real blood-royal of England.

What are we to conclude? Is it that all
Englishmen would be found cousins within four
centuries if we could all trace our trees? Or is
it true that certain small "connections" have
produced eminent characters out of all proportion to their size? Mr. Gun does not help us
to a scientific conclusion, but it will be a very
cautious and sceptical reader who does not leave
his book with a bias for the latter conclusion.

TROTSKY ON ENGLAND

A CONTEMPORARY reviewing this book[1] says: "He stammers out platitudes in the voice of a phonograph with a scratched record." I should guess that Trotsky dictated it. In its English dress it emerges in a turbid stream with a hectoring gurgle which is characteristic of modern revolutionary literature translated from the Russian. Its dogmatic tone about our affairs, where even the author's flashes of insight are clouded by his inevitable ignorance of what he is talking about, cannot commend it to an English reader. Yet there is a certain style about Trotsky. A personality is visible through the distorting medium. And it is not all platitudes.

The book is, first of all, an attack on the official leaders of the British Labour Party because of their "religiosity," and because they believe that it is useful to prepare for Socialism without preparing for Revolution at the same time. Trotsky sees, what is probably true, that

[1] L. Trotsky, *Where is Britain Going?*

84

our Labour Party is the direct offspring of the
Radical Nonconformists and the philanthropic
bourgeois, without a tinge of atheism, blood,
and revolution. Emotionally and intellectually,
therefore, he finds them intensely unsympathetic.
A short anthology will exhibit his state of mind:

The doctrine of the leaders of the Labour Party is a
kind of amalgam of Conservatism and Liberalism, par-
tially adapted to the needs of trade unions. . . . The
Liberal and semi-Liberal leaders of the Labour Party
still think that the social revolution is the mournful
privilege of the European Continent.

"In the realm of feeling and conscience," Mac-
Donald begins, "in the realm of spirit, Socialism forms
the religion of service to the people." In those words is
immediately betrayed the benevolent bourgeois, the left
Liberal, who "serves" the people, coming to them from
one side, or more truly from above. Such an approach
has its roots entirely in the dim past, when the radical
intelligentsia went to live in the working-class districts
of London in order to carry on cultural and educational
work.

Together with theological literature, Fabianism is
perhaps the most useless, and in any case the most boring
form of verbal creation. . . . The cheaply optimistic
Victorian epoch, when it seemed that to-morrow would
be a little better than to-day, and the day after to-morrow
still better than to-morrow, found its most finished expression in the Webbs, Snowden, MacDonald, and other
Fabians. . . . These bombastic authorities, pedants,
arrogant and ranting poltroons, systematically poison

the Labour Movement, befog the consciousness of the proletariat, and paralyse its will. . . . The Fabians, the I.L.P.ers, the Conservative bureaucrats of the trade unions represent at the moment the most counter-revolutionary force in Great Britain, and perhaps of all the world's development. . . . Fabianism, Mac-Donaldism, Pacifism, is the chief rallying-point of British imperialism and of the European, if not the world, bourgeoisie. At any cost, these self-satisfied ped-ants, these gabbling eclectics, these sentimental career-ists, these upstart liveried lackeys of the bourgeoisie, must be shown in their natural form to the workers. To reveal them as they are will mean their hopeless discrediting.

Well, that is how the gentlemen who so much alarm Mr. Winston Churchill strike the real article. And we must hope that the real article, having got it off his chest, feels better. How few words need changing, let the reader note, to permit the attribution of my anthology to the philo-fisticuffs of the Right. And the reason for this similarity is evident. Trotsky is concerned in these passages with an attitude towards public affairs, not with ultimate aims. He is just exhibiting the temper of the band of brigand-statesmen to whom Action means War, and who are irritated to fury by the atmosphere of sweet reasonableness, of charity, tolerance, and mercy in which, though the wind whistles in the East or in the South, Mr. Baldwin and

Lord Oxford and Mr. MacDonald smoke the pipe of peace. "They smoke Peace where there should be no Peace," Fascists and Bolshevists cry in a chorus, "canting, imbecile emblems of decay, senility, and death, the antithesis of Life and the Life-Force which exist only in the spirit of merciless struggle." If only it was so easy! If only one could accomplish by roaring, whether roaring like a lion or like any sucking dove!

The roaring occupies the first half of Trotsky's book. The second half, which affords a summary exposition of his political philosophy, deserves a closer attention.

First proposition. The historical process necessitates the change-over to Socialism if civilisation is to be preserved. "Without a transfer to Socialism all our culture is threatened with decay and decomposition."

Second proposition. It is unthinkable that this change-over can come about by peaceful argument and voluntary surrender. Except in response to force, the possessing classes will surrender nothing. The strike is already a resort to force. "The class struggle is a continual sequence of open or masked forces, which are regulated in more or less degree by the State, which in turn represents the organised apparatus of force of the stronger of the anta-

gonists, in other words, the ruling class." The
hypothesis that the Labour Party will come
into power by constitutional methods and will
then "proceed to the business so cautiously, so
tactfully, so intelligently, that the bourgeoisie
will not feel any need for active opposition," is
"facetious"—though this "is indeed the very
rock-bottom hope of MacDonald and company."

Third proposition.   Even if, sooner or later,
the Labour Party achieve power by constitutional methods, *the reactionary parties will at once
proceed to force*.   The possessing classes will do
lip-service to parliamentary methods so long as
they are in control of the parliamentary machine,
but if they are dislodged, then, Trotsky main-
tains, it is absurd to suppose that they will prove
squeamish about a resort to force on their side.
Suppose, he says, that a Labour majority in
Parliament were to decide in the most legal
fashion to confiscate the land without compensation, to put a heavy tax on capital, and to abolish
the Crown and the House of Lords, "there
cannot be the least doubt that the possessing
classes will not submit without a struggle, the
more so as all the police, judiciary, and military
apparatus is entirely in their hands."   Moreover, they control the banks and the whole
system of social credit and the machinery of
transport and trade, so that the daily food of

London, including that of the Labour Government itself, depends on the great capitalist combines. It is obvious, Trotsky argues, that these terrific means of pressure "will be brought into action with frantic violence in order to dam the activity of the Labour Government, to paralyse its exertions, to frighten it, to effect cleavages in its parliamentary majority, and, finally, to cause a financial panic, provision difficulties, and lock-outs." To suppose, indeed, that the destiny of Society is going to be determined by whether Labour achieves a parliamentary majority and not by the actual balance of material forces at the moment is an "enslavement to the fetishism of parliamentary arithmetic."

Fourth proposition. In view of all this, whilst it may be good strategy to aim also at constitutional power, it is silly not to organise on the basis that material force will be the determining factor in the end.

In the revolutionary struggle only the greatest determination is of avail to strike the arms out of the hands of reaction, to limit the period of civil war, and to lessen the number of its victims. If this course be not taken it is better not to take to arms at all. If arms are not resorted to, it is impossible to organise a general strike; if the general strike is renounced, there can be no thought of any serious struggle.

Granted his assumptions, much of Trotsky's argument is, I think, unanswerable. Nothing can be sillier than to *play* at revolution—if that is what he means. But what are his assumptions? He assumes that the moral and intellectual problems of the transformation of Society have been already solved—that a plan exists, and that nothing remains except to put it into operation. He assumes further that Society is divided into two parts—the proletariat who are converted to the plan, and the rest who for purely selfish reasons oppose it. He does not understand that no plan could win until it had first convinced many people, and that, if there really were a plan, it would draw support from many different quarters. He is so much occupied with means that he forgets to tell us what it is all for. If we pressed him, I suppose he would mention Marx. And there we will leave him with an echo of his own words— "together with theological literature, perhaps the most useless, and in any case the most boring form of verbal creation."

Trotsky's book must confirm us in our conviction of the uselessness, the empty-headedness of Force at the present stage of human affairs. Force would settle nothing—no more in the Class War than in the Wars of Nations or in the Wars of Religion. An understanding of the

historical process, to which Trotsky is so fond
of appealing, declares not for, but against,
Force at this juncture of things. We lack more
than usual a coherent scheme of progress, a
tangible ideal. All the political parties alike
have their origins in past ideas and not in new
ideas—and none more conspicuously so than
the Marxists. It is not necessary to debate the
subtleties of what justifies a man in promoting
his gospel by force; for no one has a gospel.
The next move is with the head, and fists must
wait.

March 1926.

II

LIVES OF ECONOMISTS

(Dedicated to Mary Paley Marshall, great-granddaughter of William Paley and wife of Alfred Marshall)

ROBERT MALTHUS [1]

THE FIRST OF THE CAMBRIDGE
ECONOMISTS

BACCHUS—when an Englishman is called
Bacchus—derives from Bakehouse. Similarly
the original form of the rare and curious name
of Malthus was Malthouse. The pronuncia-

[1] This biographical sketch does not pretend to collect the
available material for that definitive biography of Malthus, for
which we have long waited vainly from the pen of Dr. Bonar.
I have made free use of the common authorities—Bishop Otter's
Life prefixed to the second (posthumous) edition of Malthus's
Political Economy in 1836, W. Empson's review of Otter's edition
in the *Edinburgh Review*, January 1837, and Dr. Bonar's *Malthus
and his Work* (1st ed., 1885, preceded by the sketch "Parson
Malthus" in 1881 and followed by a 2nd ed., with the biographical chapter expanded in 1924, to which edition my subsequent
references relate) ; and I have added such other details as I have
come across in miscellaneous reading which has been neither
systematic nor exhaustive. Nor have I attempted any complete
summary or assessment of Malthus's contributions to Political
Economy, which would require a closer acquaintance than I possess
with the work of his contemporaries. My object has been to
select those items of information which seemed most to contribute
to a portrait, and, in particular, to enlarge a little on the intellectual
atmosphere in which he grew up, at home and at Cambridge.

tion of English proper names has been more constant one century with another than their spelling, which fluctuates between phonetic and etymological influences, and can generally be inferred with some confidence from an examination of the written variations. On this test (Malthus, Mawtus, Malthous, Malthouse, Mauthus, Maltus, Maultous) there can be little doubt that *Maultus*, with the first vowel as in brewer's malt and the *h* doubtfully sounded, is what we ought to say.

We need not trace the heredity of Robert Malthus [1] further back than to the Reverend Robert Malthus who became Vicar of Northolt under Cromwell and was evicted at the Restoration. Calamy calls him "an ancient divine, a man of strong reason, and mighty in the Scriptures, of great eloquence and fervour, though defective in elocution." But his parishioners thought him "a very unprofitable and fruitless minister," perhaps because he was strict in the exaction of tithes, and in a petition for his removal complained of him as having "uttered invective expressions against our army while they were in Scotland," and

[1] For a complete collection relating to records of all persons bearing this family name, *vide* J. O. Payne, *Collections for a History of the Family of Malthus*, 110 copies privately printed, 4to, in 1890. Mr. Sraffa possesses Mr. Payne's own copy of this book with additional notes and illustrations inserted.

also that "Mr. Malthus is one who hath not only a low voice but a very great impediment in his utterance"; from which it seems probable that he shared with his great-great-grandson not only the appellation of the Reverend Robert Malthus, but also the defect of a cleft palate. His son Daniel was appointed apothecary to King William by favour of the celebrated Dr. Sydenham and afterwards to Queen Anne,[1] and became a man of sufficient substance for his widow to own a coach and horses. Daniel's son Sydenham further improved the family fortunes, being a clerk in Chancery, a director of the South Sea Company, rich enough to give his daughter a dowry of £5000, and the proprietor of several landed properties in the Home Counties and Cambridgeshire.[2]

The golden mediocrity of a successful English middle-class family being now attained, Sydenham's son Daniel, our hero's father, found himself in a position of what is known in England as "independence" and decided to take advantage of it. He was educated at Queen's College,

[1] Robert Malthus's mother was a granddaughter of Thomas Graham, apothecary to George I. and George II.

[2] Sydenham Malthus bought an estate at Little Shelford, near Cambridge, for £2200. His son is recorded as possessing a number of farms in the near neighbourhood of Cambridge—at Hauxton, Newton, and Harston.

H

Oxford, but took no degree, "travelled much in Europe and in every part of this island," settled down in a pleasant neighbourhood, led the life of a small English country gentleman, cultivated intellectual tastes and friendships, wrote a few anonymous pieces,[1] and allowed diffidence to overmaster ambition. It is recorded that he "possessed the most pleasing manners with the most benevolent heart, which was experienced by all the poor wherever he lived."[2] When he died the *Gentleman's Magazine* (February 1800, p. 177) was able to record that he was "an eccentric character in the strictest sense of the term."

In 1759 Daniel Malthus had purchased a "small elegant mansion" near Dorking "known by the name of Chert-gate Farm, and taking advantage of its beauties, hill and dale, wood and water, displaying them in their naked simplicity, converted it into a gentleman's seat,

---

[1] He was the translator of Gerardin's *Essay on Landscape*, published by Dodsley in 1783. T. R. M. wrote to the *Monthly Magazine* of February 19, 1800, indignantly protesting that his father never published translations (*vide* Otter's *Life, op. cit.* p. xxii). I take the above, however, from a note written in a copy of the book in question in Malthus's own library.

[2] Manning and Bray, *History of Surrey*. (Bray was Daniel Malthus's son-in-law.) A charming pastel picture of a boy in blue, now hanging in Mr. Robert Malthus's house at Albury, is reputed by family tradition to be a portrait of Daniel Malthus.

giving it the name of The Rookery." [1]   Here
on February 13,[2] 1766, was born Thomas
Robert Malthus, his second son, the author of
the *Essay on the Principle of Population*. When
the babe was three weeks old, on March 9,
1766, two fairy godmothers, Jean-Jacques
Rousseau and David Hume, called together at
The Rookery,[3] and may be presumed to have
assigned to the infant with a kiss diverse
intellectual gifts.

For Daniel Malthus was not only a friend
of Hume,[4] but a devoted, not to say passionate,

[1] Manning and Bray, *op. cit.* In 1768 Daniel Malthus sold
The Rookery and the family moved to a less extensive establishment at Albury, not far from Guildford. An early engraving
of The Rookery is inserted in Mr. Sraffa's copy of Mr. Payne's
book (*vide supra*), and the house is still standing, though with
some changes. It was a substantial and expensive essay in Gothi-
cism—another testimony to the contemporary intellectual influences in which Daniel Malthus was interested. Albury House, not
to be confused with the Duke of Northumberland's Albury Park
nor with either of the two houses in Albury now owned by the
Malthus family (Dalton Hill and The Cottage), is no longer
standing. An engraving alleged to represent it is inserted in
Mr. Sraffa's copy of Mr. Payne's book.

[2] See Wotton Parish Registers.

[3] *Vide* Greig, *Letters of David Hume*, vol. ii. p. 24.

[4] See Hume's letters of March 2 and March 27, 1766, Nos.
309 and 315 in Dr. Greig's edition (*op. cit.*). Dr. Bonar reports
(*op. cit.* 2nd. ed. p. 402) a family tradition, on the authority of
the late Colonel Sydenham Malthus, that Daniel Malthus also
corresponded with Voltaire, but that "a lady into whose hands
the letters came gave them to the flames." The correspondence
with Rousseau shows that D. M. was also acquainted with Wilkes,

admirer of Rousseau. When Rousseau first
came to England, Hume endeavoured to settle
him in Surrey in the near neighbourhood of
Daniel Malthus, who, "desirous of doing him
every kind of service," would have provided
congenial company and kept upon him a
benevolent eye.[1] Like most of Hume's good
intentions towards his uneasy visitant, the
project broke down. The cottage at the foot
of Leith Hill pointed out to Fanny Burney
in later years as *l'asile de Jean-Jacques* [2] was
never occupied by him, but was, doubtless, the
retreat which Daniel Malthus had fixed upon
as suitable and Jean-Jacques had inspected [3]
on March 8, 1766, but afterwards rejected.
A fortnight later Rousseau had begun his
disastrous sojourn at Wootton [4] in the Peak of

who visited him at The Rookery and from whom he first heard
of the story of the quarrel between Rousseau and Hume.

[1] An excellent account of the episode is to be found in Courtois'
Le Séjour de Jean-Jacques Rousseau en Angleterre (1911).

[2] Vide *Diary and Letters of Mme. D'Arblay* (Dobson's edition),
vol. v. p. 145. Miss Burney refers to D. M. as "Mr. Malthouse."

[3] Rousseau writes to Malthus on January 2, 1767: "Je pense
souvent avec plaisir à la ferme solitaire que nous avons vue en-
semble et à l'avantage d'y être votre voisin; mais ceci sont plutôt
des souhaits vagues que des projets d'une prochaine exécution."

[4] Lent by Mr. Richard Davenport. It was here that Rousseau
began to write the *Confessions*. One of the refuges almost selected
by Rousseau on his visit to Malthus was the other Wotton,
Evelyn's Wotton in Surrey, very near to Albury (see Daniel
Malthus's letter of March 12, 1766, where he explains that he has
been approaching Sir John Evelyn on the matter).

Derbyshire, where, cold and bored and lonely, he brewed within a few weeks his extraordinary quarrel with Hume.[1]

This most famous of literary *causes* might never have occurred, I think, if only Jean-Jacques had accepted Daniel Malthus's most pressing invitation. For he would have had affection poured out upon him, and have been amused and within reach. Daniel Malthus's passionate declarations of devotion to Jean-Jacques were, probably, the only occasion in his life in which his reserves were fully broken down.[2] I think that they met three times only, —when Malthus paid a tourist's visit to Môtiers in the spring of 1764, when Hume brought Rousseau to The Rookery in March 1766, and

---

[1] Of course Jean-Jacques was in the wrong. But, all the same, Hume might have shown a serener spirit, taking Adam Smith's advice " not to think of publishing anything to the world." After the superb character sketch of his guest which he wrote to Dr. Blair on March 21, 1766 (Greig, No. 314), showing so deep an understanding, his later letters (as also the *Concise and Genuine Account*, published in 1766, fascinating though it is in itself) are the product, not of a comprehending heart, but of an extreme anxiety to avoid a scandal which his Paris friends might misunderstand.

[2] When Rousseau fails to answer a letter, Daniel Malthus (December 4, 1767) breaks out: "Est-il possible, Monsieur, que vous ayez reçu ma lettre, et que vous me refusiez les deux mots que je vous demandois ? Je ne veux pas le croire. Je ne donne pas une fausse importance à mon amitié. Ne me respectez pas mais respectez-vous vous-même. Vous laissez dans le cœur d'un être semblable au votre une idée affligeante que vous pouvez ôter, le cœur qui vous aime si tendrement ne sait pas vous accuser."

when Malthus travelled up to see him at Wootton in June of the same year. But to judge from thirteen letters from Malthus to Rousseau, which have been preserved, and one from Rousseau to Malthus,[1] the meetings were a great success. Malthus worshipped Jean-Jacques, and Jean-Jacques was cordial and friendly in return, speaking of "les sentiments d'estime et d'attachement que vous m'avez inspirés," and of Malthus's "hospitalité si douce." Malthus was even able to defend the character of Hume without becoming embroiled in the quarrel. There are many references to their botanising together, and Rousseau complains what a nuisance it is that he cannot identify the names of what he sees on his walks in Derbyshire; for he needs, he says, "une occupation qui demande de l'exercice; car rien ne me fait tant de mal que de rester assis, ou d'écrire ou lire." Later on (in 1768) we find

---

[1] Malthus's letters were printed by Courtois, *op. cit.*, and are Nos. 2908, 2915, 2939, 2940, 2941, 2952, 2953 (to Mlle. le Vasseur), 2970, 2979, 3073, 3182, 3440 in the *Correspondance générale de Rousseau*, to which must be added letters of December 14, 1767, and January 24, 1768, which the *Correspondance générale* has not yet reached. Rousseau's letter is No. 3211, and is a discovery of M. Courtois, having been wrongly assumed by previous editors to be addressed to another correspondent. It appears that the correspondence was resumed in 1770 and that the two remained in touch. But the later letters were not found by M. Courtois. It remains to be seen if the later volumes of the *Correspondance générale* (not yet published) will disclose anything.

Daniel Malthus taking great pains to complete
Rousseau's botanical library for him, at a time
when Rousseau was probably contemplating his
Letters to a Lady on the Elements of Botany, which
were dated 1771; and two years later Rousseau,
who had a craze for dispossessing himself of
his books from time to time, sold the whole
library back to Malthus, adding to it the gift
of a part of his herbarium.[1] These books reappear in Daniel Malthus's will, where we find
the following provision: "To Mrs. Jane
Dalton [2] I give all my botanical books in which
the name of Rousseau is written and a box of
plants given me by Mons. Rousseau." Two
of these books are still to be found in the
library of Dalton Hill, Albury, now owned by
Mr. Robert Malthus,[3] namely, Ray's *Synopsis*

[1] *Vide* Courtois, *op. cit.* p. 99.

[2] A niece of Daniel Malthus's mother, referred to by Daniel
Malthus in a letter to Rousseau as "la petite cousine qui est botaniste
à toute outrance," who evidently shared the botanical tastes of
Daniel Malthus and Rousseau, and is recorded as having presented
Rousseau with a copy of *Johnson sur Gerard* (presumably Gerarde's
Herball, 1633) from her own library when Daniel Malthus was
unable to get one through the booksellers. (See Daniel Malthus's
letter to Rousseau, January 24, 1768, printed by Courtois, *op.
cit.* p. 219.) Those who are curious to explore the extensive
cousinage of the Malthuses are recommended to consult Mr.
Payne's book and preferably Mr. Sraffa's copy of it. They were
in the habit, almost as often as not, of marrying their cousins (T.
R. Malthus himself married his cousin), and the result is unusually
complicated.

[3] A great-grandson of Sydenham Malthus, the elder brother of

methodica stirpium Brittanicarum and de Sauvage's *Méthode pour connoître les plantes par les
feuilles*, both inscribed with the name of
Rousseau and heavily scored.[1]

Otter relates that Daniel Malthus was a
literary executor of Rousseau. This seems im-
probable.[2] But Daniel Malthus's loyalty lasted
to the end, and he subscribed for six copies, at
a cost of thirty guineas, of Rousseau's post-

T. R. Malthus. The only other living descendants of Daniel
Malthus in the male line are, I think, settled in New Zealand.
T. R. Malthus, who had three children, has no living descendants.
There must, however, be many descendants of Daniel Malthus
in the female line. According to Mr. Payne's records (*op. cit.*)
Daniel had eight children, and at least nineteen grandchildren,
whilst it would seem that his great-grandchildren must have
considerably exceeded thirty. I cannot count the present
generation of great-great-grandchildren. There would appear,
however, to be a safe margin for the operation of the geometrical
law! The most distinguished of Daniel's living or recently living
descendants are the Brays of Shere near Albury, to which the late
Mr. Justice Bray belonged.

[1] This library, still preserved intact at Dalton Hill, is the library
of the Reverend Henry Malthus, T. R. Malthus's son. It includes,
however, a considerable part of T. R. Malthus's library, as well as
a number of books from Daniel's library. Dr. Bonar has had
prepared a complete and careful catalogue of the whole collection.
It is to him that I am indebted for the opportunity to obtain these
particulars.

[2] Perhaps the later volumes of the *Correspondance générale* will
throw some light on it. Rousseau, it is true, executed a will
during his stay in England, and Malthus may have been mentioned in it. Mr. Sraffa suggests to me that Otter may have
been misled by the fact that, shortly before his death, Rousseau
entrusted the manuscript of the *Confessions* to Paul Moultou.

humous *Consolations des misères de ma vie.*
And now in these few pages I piously fulfil his
wish: "Si jamais je suis connu, ce seroit sous
le nom de l'ami de Rousseau."

There is a charming account of Daniel's way
of life in his letter to Rousseau of January 24,
1768.[1] In the summer botanising walks,

ma chère Henriette et ses enfants en prenoient leur
part, et nous fûmes quelque fois une famille herbori-
sante, couchée sur la pente de cette colline que peut-
être vous vous rappelez. . . . L'hiver un peu de
lecture (je sens déjà l'effet de votre lettre, car je me
suis saisi de l'*Émile*). Je fais des grandes promenades
avec mes enfants. Je passe plus de temps dans les
chaumières que dans les châteaux du voisinage. Il y a
toujours à s'employer dans une ferme et à faire des
petites expériences. Je chasse le renard, ce qui je
fais en partie par habitude, et en partie de ce que cela
amuse mon imagination de quelque idée de vie sauvage.

With this delightful thought our gentle fox-
hunting squire could picture himself as Rousseau's Noble Savage.

As a friend of the author of the *Émile*, Daniel
Malthus was disposed to experiments in education; and Robert, showing a promise which
awakened his father's love and ambition, was
educated privately, partly by Daniel himself
and partly by tutors. The first of these was
Richard Graves, "a gentleman of considerable

---

[1] Courtois, *op. cit.* p. 221.

learning and humour," a friend of Shenstone
and author of *The Spiritual Quixote*, a satire on
the Methodists. At sixteen he was transferred
to Gilbert Wakefield, an heretical clergyman,
" wild, restless and paradoxical in many of his
opinions, a prompt and hardy disputant," a
correspondent of Charles Fox and a disciple of
Rousseau, who stated his principles of education
thus :

The greatest service of tuition to any youth is to
teach him the exercise of his own powers, to conduct
him to the limits of knowledge by that gradual process
in which he sees and secures his own way, and rejoices
in a consciousness of his own faculties and his own
proficiency.[1]

In 1799, Wakefield was imprisoned in Dor-
chester gaol for expressing a wish that the
French revolutionaries would invade and conquer England.

Some schoolboy letters of Robert Malthus
still extant [2] show that he was much attached
to Wakefield. Wakefield had been a Fellow of
Jesus College, Cambridge; and as a consequence
of this connection Robert Malthus, the first of
the Cambridge economists, came up to Jesus as
a pensioner in the winter term of 1784, being

---

[1] *Life of Gilbert Wakefield*, vol. i. p. 344, quoted by Dr. Bonar,
op. cit. p. 405.

[2] Colonel Sydenham Malthus, the father of the present owner,
put them at Dr. Bonar's disposal.

eighteen years of age. On November 14, 1784, he wrote home as follows:

I am now pretty well settled in my rooms. The lectures begin to-morrow; and, as I had time last week to look over my mathematics a little, I was, upon examination yesterday, found prepared to read with the year above me. We begin with mechanics and Maclaurin, Newton, and Keill's *Physics*. We shall also have lectures on Mondays and Fridays in Duncan's *Logick*, and in Tacitus's *Life of Agricola* on Wednesdays and Saturdays. I have subscribed to a bookseller who has supplied me with all the books necessary. We have some clever men at college, and I think it seems rather the fashion to read. The chief study is mathematics, for all honour in taking a degree depends upon that science, and the great aim of most of the men is to take an honourable degree. At the same time I believe we have some good classics. I am acquainted with two, one of them in this year, who is indeed an exceedingly clever man and will stand a very good chance for the classical prize if he does not neglect himself. I have read in chapel twice.

His expenses came to £100 a year. If it rose higher, Daniel Malthus wrote, the clergy could not go on sending their sons to college; abroad at Leipzig it could be done for £25.[1]

At this time the University was just stirring from a long sleep, and Jesus, which had been among the sleepiest, was becoming a centre of

---

[1] Quoted by Bonar, *op. cit.* p. 408.

intellectual ferment.   Malthus probably owes
as much to the intellectual company he kept
during his years at Jesus as to the influence
and sympathy of his father.   His tutor,
William Frend, who had been a pupil of Paley's
and was an intimate of Priestley's, became
in Malthus's third year (1787) the centre of
one of the most famous of University controversies, through his secession from the
Church of England and his advocacy of Uni-
tarianism, freedom of thought, and pacifism.
Paley [1] himself had left Cambridge in 1775,
but his *Principles of Moral and Political Philosophy*, or, as it was originally called, the *Principles of Morality and Politics*, was published in
Malthus's first year (1785) at Cambridge, and
must be placed high,[2] I think, amongst the

[1] I wish I could have included some account of Paley amongst
these Essays.   For Paley, so little appreciated now, was for a
generation or more an intellectual influence on Cambridge
only second to Newton.   Perhaps, in a sense, *he* was the first
of the Cambridge economists.   If anyone will take up again
Paley's *Principles* he will find, contrary perhaps to his expecta-
tions, an immortal book.   Or glance through G. W. Meadley's
Memoirs of William Paley for a fascinating account of the lovable
wit and eccentricities of a typical Cambridge don.   His great-
granddaughter, Mrs. Alfred Marshall, has shown me a little
embroidered case containing the Archdeacon's (very businesslike)
love letters.

[2] Though Dr. Bonar thinks that Malthus "preferred where he
could to draw rather from Tucker than from Paley" (*op. cit.* p.
324).   Abraham Tucker, author of the *Light of Nature*, had been
for many years a near neighbour of Daniel Malthus at Dorking.

Eco. Conseq. of the Peace

HC
57
.K4

DASA's in Bios.
574
.A1K4

Mantoux, Étienne
The Carthaginian Peace
or The Eco. Conseq.
of Mr. Keynes.
330.904
M293ca

intellectual influences on the author of the
Essay on Population.[1]   Moreover, he found
himself in a small group of brilliant undergraduates of whom Bishop Otter, his bio-
grapher, and E. D. Clarke, traveller, Cambridge
eccentric, and professor, may be chiefly named.
After Malthus had taken his B.A. degree
Coleridge entered the College (in 1791).   When
the young Coleridge occupied the ground-floor
room on the right hand of the staircase facing
the great gate, Jesus cannot have been a dull
place—unending conversation rolling out across
the Court:

> As erst when from the Muses' calm abode
> I came, with Learning's meed not unbestow'd:
> When as she twin'd a laurel round my brow,
> And met my kiss, and half returned my vow.[2]

"What evenings have I spent in those rooms!"
wrote a contemporary.[3]   "What little suppers, or
sizings, as they were called, have I enjoyed, when
Aeschylus and Plato and Thucydides were pushed

---

[1] As also on Bentham, a contemporary of Malthus, with whom,
however, there is no record of his having been in contact.

[2] "An Effusion on an Autumnal Evening," written by
Coleridge "in early youth."   It is hard to read without a tear
these tender and foreboding lines which end:

> Mine eye the gleam pursues with wistful gaze:
> Sees shades on shades with deeper tint impend,
> Till chill and damp the moonless night descend.

[3] C. W. L. Grice, *Gentleman's Magazine* (1834), quoted by
Gray, *Jesus College*.

aside with a pile of lexicons, to discuss the pamphlets of the day. Ever and anon a pamphlet issued from the pen of Burke. There was no need of having the book before us. Coleridge had read it in the morning, and in the evening he would repeat whole pages *verbatim*. Frend's trial was then in progress. Pamphlets swarmed from the Press. Coleridge had read them all; and in the evening, with our negus, we had them *vivâ-voce* gloriously."

As Malthus succeeded to a fellowship in June 1793 he was one of those who passed the following order on December 19, 1793:

Agreed, that if Coleridge, who has left College without leave, should not return within a month from this day, and pay his debts to his tutor, or give reasonable security that they should be paid, his name be taken off the Boards.

Coleridge, it seems, had enlisted in the 15th Dragoons in the assumed name of Silas Tomkins Comberbacke. I must not be further drawn into the career of Coleridge at Jesus,[1] but on his return from this escapade he was sentenced to a month's confinement to the precincts of the College, and to translate the works of Deme-

---

[1] Coleridge's Unitarian period was under the influence of Frend. Shortly after he went down Coleridge "announced himself to preach in the Unitarian Chapel at Bath as 'The Rev. S. T. Coleridge of Jesus College, Cambridge,' and to mark his severance from the 'gentlemen in black,' so much reprobated in Frend's tract, performed that office in blue coat and white waistcoat" (Gray, *Jesus College*, p. 180).

trius Phalereus into English. Coleridge's later violence against the *Essay on Population* is well known:

Finally, behold this mighty nation, its rulers and its wise men listening—to Paley and—to Malthus! It is mournful, mournful [*Literary Remains of Samuel Taylor Coleridge*, p. 328].

I solemnly declare that I do not believe that all the heresies and sects and factions, which the ignorance and the weakness and the wickedness of man have ever given birth to, were altogether so disgraceful to man as a Christian, a philosopher, a statesman, or citizen, as this abominable tenet [*Table Talk*, p. 88].[1]

At College Robert Malthus is said to have been fond of cricket and skating, obtained prizes for Latin and English Declamations, was elected Brunsell Exhibitioner in the College in 1786, and graduated as Ninth Wrangler in 1788. In an undergraduate letter home, just before achieving his Wranglership, he writes of himself as reading Gibbon and looking forward to the last three volumes, which were to come out a few months later:

I have been lately reading Gibbon's *Decline of the Roman Empire*. He gives one some useful information concerning the origin and progress of those nations of

---

[1] Coleridge's main criticisms are to be found in manuscript marginal comments on his copy of the second edition of the *Essay on Population* now in the British Museum. See Bonar, *op. cit.* p. 371.

barbarians which now form the polished states of Europe, and throws some light upon the beginning of that dark period which so long overwhelmed the world, and which cannot, I think, but excite one's curiosity.   He is a very entertaining writer in my opinion; his style is sometimes really sublime, everywhere interesting and agreeable, though perhaps it may in general be call'd rather too florid for history.   I shall like much to see his next volumes [April 17, 1788].[1]

In later life Malthus's mildness and gentleness of temper and of demeanour may have been excessive,[2] but at Cambridge he was a gay companion.   His humorous quality, says Otter, was prevalent throughout his youth, and even survived a portion of his manhood, and at Cambridge in particular, set off as it used to be by a very comic expression of features, and a most peculiar intonation of voice when he was in the vein, was often a source of infinite delight and pleasantry to his companions.

But even as an undergraduate he was particularly distinguished, according to Otter, by a degree of temperance and prudence, very rare at that period, and carried by him even into his academical

---

[1] Bonar, *op. cit.* p. 412.

[2] The obituary writer in the *Gentleman's Magazine* (1835, p. 325) records that one (doubtless Otter) "who has known him intimately for nearly fifty years scarcely ever saw him ruffled, *never* angry, never above measure elated or depressed.   He had this felicity of mind, almost peculiar to himself, that, being singularly alive to the approbation of the wise and good, and anxious generally for the regard of his fellow creatures, he was impassive to unmerited abuse."

pursuits. In these he was always more remarkable for the steadiness than for the ardour of his application, preferring to exert his mind equally in the various departments of literature then cultivated in the College rather than to devote it exclusively or eminently to any one.

On June 10, 1793, when the movement for the expulsion of Frend [1] from the College was at its height, he was admitted to a fellowship, and resided irregularly until he vacated it by marriage in 1804. He had taken orders about 1788,[2] and after 1796 he divided his time between Cambridge and a curacy at Albury, near his father's house. He was instituted to the rectory of Walesby, Lincs, on Nov. 21, 1803, on the presentation of Henry Dalton, doubtless a relative, and held it as a non-resident incumbent for the rest of his life, leaving the parish in charge of a succession of curates.[3]

[1] "On the last day of 1792 Tom Paine's effigy was burnt by the mob on the Market Hill at Cambridge" (Gray, *Jesus College* p. 171). Frend's pamphlet, *Peace and Union recommended to the Associated Bodies of Republicans and Anti-Republicans*, was published two months later. Frend became Secretary and Actuary of the Rock Assurance Company and, dying in 1841, outlived Malthus and all his other contemporaries (Gray, *loc. cit.*).

[2] Two years before he had consulted the head of his College about this, particularly as to whether the defect in his speech would stand in the way. But when he explained that "the utmost of his wishes was a retired living in the country," Dr. Beadon withdrew any objection (*vide* T. R. M.'s letter to Daniel Malthus, April 19, 1786, printed by Dr. Bonar, *op. cit.* p. 409).

[3] I am indebted for this information to Canon Foster of the Lincoln Record Society. The living seems to have been a good one.

I

A few letters written by Daniel Malthus to his son, when the latter was an undergraduate at Jesus, were printed by Otter in his *Memoir*. The following from a letter written by his father to Robert Malthus on his election to a fellowship must be quoted in full for the light it casts on their relationship:

I heartily congratulate you upon your success; it gives me a sort of pleasure which arises from my own regrets. The things which I have missed in life, I should the more sensibly wish for you.

Alas! my dear Bob, I have no right to talk to you of idleness, but when I wrote that letter to you with which you were displeased, I was deeply impressed with my own broken purposes and imperfect pursuits; I thought I foresaw in you, from the memory of my own youth, the same tendency to lose the steps you had gained, with the same disposition to self-reproach, and I wished to make my unfortunate experience of some use to you. It was, indeed, but little that you wanted it, which made me the more eager to give it you, and I wrote to you with more tenderness of heart than I would in general pretend to, and committed myself in a certain manner which made your answer a rough disappointment to me, and it drove me back into myself. You have, as you say, worn out that impression, and you have a good right to have done it; for I have seen in you the most unexceptionable character, the sweetest manners, the most sensible and the kindest conduct, always above *throwing little stones into my garden*, which you know I don't easily forgive, and uniformly making everybody easy and amused about you. Nothing can have been wanting to what, if I were the most fretful and fastidious, I could have required in a companion; and nothing even to my wishes for your happiness, but where they were either whimsical, or unreasonable, or most likely mistaken. I have often been on the point of taking hold of your hand and bursting into tears at the time that I was refusing you my affections: my approbation I was precipitate to give you.

Write to me, if I could do anything about your church, and you want any thing to be done for you, such as I am, believe me, dear Bob, yours most affectionately,   Daniel Malthus

Malthus's first essay in authorship, *The Crisis, a View of the Recent Interesting State of Great Britain by a Friend to the Constitution*, written in 1796, in his thirtieth year, in criticism of Pitt's administration, failed to find a publisher. Extracts quoted by Otter and by Empson indicate that his interest was already aroused in the social problems of Political Economy, and even in the question of Population itself:

On the subject of population [he wrote] I cannot agree with Archdeacon Paley, who says, that the quantity of happiness in any country is best measured by the number of people. Increasing population is the most certain possible sign of the happiness and prosperity of a state; but the actual population may be only a sign of the happiness that is past.

In 1798, when Malthus was thirty-two years old, there was published anonymously *An Essay on the Principle of Population, as it affects the future improvement of Society: with remarks on the speculations of Mr. Godwin, M. Condorcet, and other writers.*

It was in conversation with Daniel Malthus that there occurred to Robert Malthus the generalisation which has made him famous. The story is well known on the authority of Bishop Otter, who had it from Malthus himself. In 1793 Godwin's *Political Justice* had appeared. In frequent discussion the father defended, and the son attacked, the doctrine of a future age of perfect equality and happiness.

And when the question had been often the subject of animated discussion between them, and the son had rested his cause, principally upon the obstacles which the tendency of population, to increase faster than the means of subsistence, would always throw in the way; he was desired to put down in writing, for maturer consideration, the substance of his argument, the consequence of which was the Essay on Population. Whether the father was converted or not we do not know, but certain it is that he was strongly impressed with the importance of the views and the ingenuity of the argument contained in the MS., and recommended his son to submit his labours to the public.

The first edition, an octavo volume of about 50,000 words, is an almost completely different, and for posterity a superior book, to the second edition of five years later in quarto, which by the fifth edition had swollen to some 250,000 words in three volumes. The first edition, written, as Malthus explains in the second edition, "on the impulse of the occasion, and from the few materials which were then within my reach in a country situation," is mainly an *a priori* work, concerned on the one hand with the refutation of the perfectibilists and on the other with the justification of the methods of the Creator, in spite of appearance to the contrary.

The first essay is not only *a priori* and philosophical in method, but it is bold and rhetorical in style with much *bravura* of language and sentiment; whereas in the later editions political philosophy gives way to political economy, general principles are overlaid by the inductive verifications of a pioneer in sociological history, and the brilliance and high spirits of a young man writing in the last years of the Directory disappear. "Verbiage and senseless repetition" is Coleridge's marginal comment in his copy of the second edition:

Are we now to have a quarto to teach us that great misery and great vice arise from poverty, and that there must be poverty in its worst shape wherever there are more mouths than loaves and more Heads than Brains?

To judge from the rarity of the book, the first edition must have been a very small one (Malthus stated in 1820 that he had not made out of his writings above £1000 altogether[1]), and we know that it went out of print almost immediately, though five years passed before it was followed by a second. But it attracted immediate attention, and the warfare of pamphlets instantly commenced (more than a score, according to Dr. Bonar, even in the five years before the second edition) which for 135 years has never ceased. The voice of objective reason had been raised against a deep instinct which the evolutionary struggle had been implanting from the commencement of life; and man's mind, in the conscious pursuit of happiness, was daring to demand the reins of government from out of the hands of the unconscious urge for mere predominant survival.

Paley himself was converted,[2] who had once argued that "the decay of population is the greatest evil a State can suffer, and the improvement of it the object which ought in all countries to be aimed at, in preference to every other political purpose whatsoever." Even the poli-

[1] Unlike Paley, who sold the first edition of his *Principles* (his first essay in authorship) for £1000.

[2] Cf. G. W. Meadley, *Memoirs of William Paley* (2nd ed.), p. 219.

ticians took note, and Otter records a meeting
between Pitt and Malthus in December
1801 :

> It happened that Mr. Pitt was at this time upon a
> sort of canvassing visit at the University. . . . At a
> supper at Jesus lodge in the company of some young
> travellers, particularly Mr. Malthus, etc., he was in-
> duced to unbend in a very easy conversation respecting
> Sir Sidney Smith, the massacre at Jaffa, the Pasha of
> Acre, Clarke, Carlisle, etc.

A year before, in dropping his new Poor Bill,
Pitt, who in 1796 thought that a man had "en-
riched his country" by producing a number
of children, even if the whole family were
paupers,[1] had stated in the House of Commons that he did so in deference to the
objections of "those whose opinions he was
bound to respect," meaning, it is said, Bentham
and Malthus.

Malthus's *Essay* is a work of youthful genius.
The author was fully conscious of the significance of the ideas he was expressing. He believed that he had found the clue to human
misery. The importance of the *Essay* con-
sisted not in the novelty of his facts but in
the smashing emphasis he placed on a simple
generalisation arising out of them. Indeed his

[1] Cf. Cannan, *History of the Theories of Production and Distribution.*

leading idea had been largely anticipated in a clumsier way by other eighteenth-century writers without attracting attention.

The book can claim a place amongst those which have had great influence on the progress of thought. It is profoundly in the English tradition of humane science—in that tradition of Scotch and English thought, in which there has been, I think, an extraordinary continuity of *feeling*, if I may so express it, from the eighteenth century to the present time—the tradition which is suggested by the names of Locke, Hume, Adam Smith, Paley, Bentham, Darwin, and Mill, a tradition marked by a love of truth and a most noble lucidity, by a prosaic sanity free from sentiment or metaphysic, and by an immense disinterestedness and public spirit. There is a continuity in these writings, not only of feeling, but of actual matter. It is in this company that Malthus belongs.

Malthus's transition from the *a priori* methods of Cambridge—whether Paley, the Mathematical Tripos, or the Unitarians—to the inductive argument of the later editions was assisted by a tour which he undertook in search of materials in 1799 "through Sweden, Norway, Finland, and a part of Russia, these being the only countries at the time open to English travellers," and another in France and Switzerland during

the short peace of 1802.[1] The northern tour
was in the company of a party of Jesus friends,
Otter, Clarke, and Cripps, of whom Malthus
and Otter, exhausted perhaps by the terrific and
eccentric energy of E. D. Clarke, by nature a
traveller and collector, performed a part only of
the journey. Clarke and Cripps continued for
a period of two or three years, returning by
Constantinople, having accumulated a number of objects of every description, many of
which now rest in the Fitzwilliam Museum.[2]
Clarke's letters, many of which are printed in
his *Life and Travels*, were read out by his stay-
at-home friends in the Combination Room at
Jesus amidst the greatest curiosity and interest.[3]
Clarke later became Senior Tutor of Jesus
(1805), first Professor of Mineralogy (1808),
and finally University Librarian (1817).

[1] In January 1800 Daniel Malthus died, aged seventy, and
three months later his wife, Robert's mother, followed him, aged
sixty-seven. They are both buried in Wotton Churchyard.

[2] His Plato from Patmos is in the Bodleian. The Professor of
History wrote:

> I sing of a Tutor renown'd
> Who went roving and raving for knowledge,
> And gathered it all the world round,
> And brought it in boxes to college.

[3] The following from Gunning's *Reminiscences* is well known:
"I recollect dining with Outram (the Public Orator) when a
packet arrived from Clarke. The first letter began with these
words: 'Here I am, eating strawberries within the Arctic Circle.'
We were so intent on his dessert that we forgot our own."

Meanwhile Malthus had continued his economic studies with a pamphlet, published anonymously (like the first edition of the *Essay*) in 1800, entitled *An Investigation of the Cause of the Present High Price of Provisions*. This pamphlet has importance both in itself and as showing that Malthus was already disposed to a certain line of approach in handling practical economic problems which he was to develop later on in his correspondence with Ricardo,—a method which to me is most sympathetic, and, as I think, more likely to lead to right conclusions than the alternative approach of Ricardo. But it was Ricardo's more fascinating intellectual construction which was victorious, and Ricardo who, by turning his back so completely on Malthus's ideas, constrained the subject for a full hundred years in an artificial groove.

According to Malthus's good common-sense notion prices and profits are primarily determined by something which he described, though none too clearly, as "effective demand." Ricardo favoured a much more rigid approach, went behind "effective demand" to the underlying conditions of money on the one hand and real costs and the real division of the product on the other hand, conceived these fundamental factors as automatically working themselves out

in a unique and unequivocal way, and looked
on Malthus's method as very superficial. But
Ricardo, in the course of simplifying the many
successive stages of his highly abstract argument, departed, necessarily and more than he
himself was aware, away from the actual facts;
whereas Malthus, by taking up the tale much
nearer its conclusion, had a firmer hold on what
may be expected to happen in the real world.
Ricardo is the father of such things as the
Quantity Theory of Money and the Purchasing
Power Parity of the Exchanges. When one has
painfully escaped from the intellectual domination of these pseudo-arithmetical doctrines,
one is able, perhaps for the first time for a
hundred years, to comprehend the real significance of the vaguer intuitions of Malthus.

Malthus's conception of "effective demand"
is brilliantly illustrated in this early pamphlet
by "an idea which struck him so strongly as he
rode on horseback from Hastings to Town"
that he stopped two days in his "garret in town,"
"sitting up till two o'clock to finish it that it
might come out before the meeting of parliament." [1]   He was pondering why the price of

---

[1] See a letter of Malthus's (November 28, 1800), published by
Prof. Foxwell in the *Economic Journal* (1897), p. 270. Malthus
records that Pitt was much impressed, and that in a Report of a
Committee of the House of Commons "much of the same kind of
reasoning has been adopted."

provisions should have risen by so much more than could be accounted for by any deficiency in the harvest.   He did not, like Ricardo a few years later, invoke the quantity of money.[1]   He found the cause in the increase in working-class *incomes* as a consequence of parish allowances being raised in proportion to the cost of living.

I am most strongly inclined to suspect, that the attempt in most parts of the kingdom to increase the parish allowances in proportion to the price of corn, combined with the riches of the country, which have enabled it to proceed as far as it has done in this attempt, is, comparatively speaking, the sole cause which has occasioned the price of provisions in this country to rise so much higher than the degree of scarcity would seem to warrant, so much higher than it would do in any other country where this cause did not operate. . . .

Let us suppose a commodity in great request by fifty people, but of which, from some failure in its production, there is only sufficient to supply forty.   If the fortieth man from the top have two shillings which he can spend in this commodity, and the thirty-nine above him, more, in various proportions, and the ten below,

---

[1] Not that Malthus neglected this factor.   He dealt with it admirably as follows: "To circulate the same, or nearly the same, quantity of commodities through a country, when they bear a much higher price, must require a greater quantity of the medium, whatever that may be. . . . If the quantity of paper, therefore, in circulation has greatly increased during the last year, I should be inclined to consider it rather as the effect than the cause of the high price of provisions.   This fulness of circulating medium, however, will be one of the obstacles in the way to returning cheapness."

all less, the actual price of the article, according to the genuine principles of trade, will be two shillings. . . . Let us suppose, now, that somebody gives the ten poor men, who were excluded, a shilling apiece. The whole fifty can now offer two shillings, the price which was before asked. According to every genuine principle of fair trading, the commodity must immediately rise. If it do not, I would ask, upon what principle are ten, out of the fifty who are all able to offer two shillings, to be rejected? For still, according to the supposition, there is only enough for forty. The two shillings of a poor man are just as good as the two shillings of a rich man; and, if we interfere to prevent the commodity from rising out of the reach of the poorest ten, whoever they may be, we must toss up, draw lots, raffle, or fight, to determine who are to be excluded. It would be beyond my present purpose to enter into the question whether any of these modes would be more eligible, for the distribution of the commodities of a country, than the sordid distinction of money; but certainly, according to the customs of all civilised and enlightened nations, and according to every principle of commercial dealing, the price must be allowed to rise to that point which will put it beyond the power of ten out of the fifty to purchase. This point will, perhaps, be half a crown or more, which will now become the price of the commodity. Let another shilling apiece be given to the excluded ten: all will now be able to offer half a crown. The price must in consequence immediately rise to three shillings or more, and so on *toties quoties*.

The words and the ideas are simple. But here is the beginning of systematic economic

thinking.   There is much else in the pamphlet
—almost the whole of it—which would bear
quotation.   This *Investigation* [1] is one of the
best things Malthus ever wrote, though there
are great passages in the *Essay*; and, now well
launched on quotation, I cannot forbear to
follow on with that famous passage from the
second edition (p. 571), in which a partly
similar idea is introduced, more magnificently
clothed, in a different context (in criticism of
Paine's *Rights of Man*):

A man who is born into a world already possessed, if
he cannot get subsistence from his parents on whom he
has a just demand, and if the society do not want his
labour, has no claim of *right* to the smallest portion of
food, and, in fact, has no business to be where he is.
At nature's mighty feast there is no vacant cover for
him.   She tells him to be gone, and will quickly execute
her own orders, if he do not work upon the compassion
of some of her guests.   If these guests get up and make
room for him, other intruders immediately appear demanding the same favour.   The report of a provision
for all that come, fills the hall with numerous claimants.
The order and harmony of the feast is disturbed, the
plenty that before reigned is changed into scarcity; and
the happiness of the guests is destroyed by the spectacle
of misery and dependence in every part of the hall, and
by the clamorous importunity of those, who are justly
enraged at not finding the provision which they had

---

[1] A scarce pamphlet, which has never, to my knowledge, been
reprinted.

been taught to expect. The guests learn too late their error, in counteracting those strict orders to all intruders, issued by the great mistress of the feast, who, wishing that all her guests should have plenty, and knowing that she could not provide for unlimited numbers, humanely refused to admit fresh comers when her table was already full.

Malthus's next pamphlet, *A Letter to Samuel Whitbread, Esq., M.P., on his Proposed Bill for the Amendment of the Poor Laws*, published in 1807, is not so happy. It is an extreme application of the principle of the *Essay on Population*. Mr. Whitbread had proposed "to empower parishes to build cottages," in short, a housing scheme, partly to remedy the appalling shortage, partly to create employment. But Malthus eagerly points out that "the difficulty of procuring habitations" must on no account be alleviated, since this is the cause why "the poor laws do not encourage early marriages so much as might naturally be expected." The poor laws raise the rates, the high level of rates prevents the building of cottages, and the deficiency of cottages mitigates the otherwise disastrous effect of the poor laws in increasing population.

Such is the tendency to form early connections, that with the encouragement of a sufficient number of tenements, I have very little doubt that the population might be so pushed and such a quantity of labour in time thrown into the market, as to render the condition of the independent labourer absolutely hopeless.

Economics is a very dangerous science.

In 1803 the new version of the *Essay on Population* appeared in a fine quarto of 600 pages priced at a guinea and a half. Up to this time Malthus had had no specific duties and was entirely free to pursue his economic inquiries. In 1804 he married.[1] In 1805, at thirty-nine years of age, he took up his appointment, made in the previous year, to the Professorship of Modern History and Political Economy at the newly founded East India College, first at Hertford and soon after at Haileybury. This was the earliest chair of

---

[1] In a footnote to *Das Kapital* (vol. i. p. 641, quoted by Dr. Bonar, *op. cit.* p. 291) Marx tells us: "Although Malthus was a clergyman of the Church of England, he had taken the monastic oath of celibacy, for this is one of the conditions of a fellowship at the Protestant University of Cambridge. By this circumstance Malthus is favourably distinguished from the other Protestant clergy, who have cast off the Catholic rule of celibacy." Not being a good Marxist scholar, I was surprised, when in 1925 I lectured before the Commissariat of Finance in Moscow, to find that any mention by me of the increase of population as being a problem for Russia was taken in ill part. But I should have remembered that Marx, criticising Malthus, had held that over-population was purely the product of a capitalist society and could not occur under Socialism. Marx's reasons for holding this view are by no means without interest, being in fact closely akin to Malthus's own theory that "effective demand" may fail in a capitalist society to keep pace with output.

Political Economy [1] to be established in England.

Malthus had now entered upon the placid existence of a scholar and teacher. He remained at Haileybury for thirty years until his death in 1834, occupying the house under the clock-turret afterwards occupied by Sir James Stephen,[2] who was the last holder of Malthus's chair. He had three children, of whom one daughter died before her maturity, and the other, Mrs. Pringle, lived on till 1885, whilst his son, the Reverend Henry Malthus, died without issue in 1882.

The *Essay* was amplified in successive editions. In 1814 and 1815 he published pamphlets on the Corn Laws, in 1815 his celebrated essay on *Rent*, and in 1820 his second book, *The Principles of Political Economy considered with a View to their Practical Application.*[3]

---

[1] The title originally proposed had been "Professor of General History, Politics, Commerce, and Finance."

[2] Leslie Stephen, who wrote the account of Malthus in the *D.N.B.*, was at that time a young don at Cambridge, chiefly noted for his feats in pedestrianism, and it is recorded that he used to think nothing of a walk from Cambridge to Haileybury to visit his father in the house long occupied by Malthus (vide *Memorials of Old Haileybury College*, p. 196). If only I had an excuse for bringing in "Old Jones"! who occupied this chair for twenty years between Malthus and Stephen, with his famous sermon: "And now, my brethren, let me ask you: which of *you* has not hatched a cockatrice's egg?"

[3] Lists of Malthus's other pamphlets, etc., are given by Otter (*op. cit.* p. xlii) and by Bonar (*op. cit.* p. 421). He also contributed

"The tradition of Mrs. Malthus's delightful evening parties, at which the élite of the London scientific world were often present, lingered at Haileybury as long as the College lasted."[1] "His servants lived with him till their marriage or settlement in life."[2] His students called him "Pop." He was a Whig; he preached sermons which dwelt especially on the goodness of the Deity; he thought Haileybury a satisfactory institution and Political Economy a suitable study for the young who "could not only understand it, but they did not even think it dull"; his sentiments were benevolent, his temper mild and easy, his nature loyal and affectionate; and he was cheerful — thus corroborating his conclusions of 1798 when he had written in the first edition of the *Essay* that "life is, generally speaking, a blessing independent of a future state . . . and we have every reason to think, that there is no more evil in the world than what is absolutely necessary as one of the ingredients in the mighty process."

The contrast between this picture and the

to the *Edinburgh* and *Quarterly Reviews*. His *Definitions of Political Economy*, published in 1827, is a minor work of no great interest (except, perhaps, his attack on Ricardo's definition of *Real Wages*).

[1] *Memorials of Old Haileybury College*, p. 199.

[2] From an obituary notice (by Otter) in the *Athenaeum*, 1835.

cruel and vicious monster of pamphleteering controversy, of which Malthus seems to have taken the least possible notice, made some of his friends indignant, but was better handled by Sydney Smith, who wrote to a correspondent in July 1821:

Philosopher Malthus came here last week. I got an agreeable party for him of unmarried people. There was only one lady who had had a child; but he is a good-natured man, and, if there are no appearances of approaching fertility, is civil to every lady. . . . Malthus is a real moral philosopher, and I would almost consent to speak as inarticulately, if I could think and act as wisely.

The *Gentleman's Magazine* (1835, p. 325) tells us in obituary language that:

In person Mr. Malthus was tall and elegantly formed; and his appearance, no less than his conduct, was that of a perfect gentleman.

The admirable portrait painted by John Linnell in 1833, now in the possession of Mr. Robert Malthus,[1] familiar through Linnell's well-known engraving of it, shows him to have been of a ruddy complexion with curling reddish or

---

[1] It hangs in the dining-room at Dalton Hill, Albury, with a companion portrait of Mrs. Malthus, also by Linnell, on the other side of the fire-place. Amongst these family pictures there is also to be found a portrait of his son, the Rev. Henry Malthus. There is a copy of the Linnell portrait at Jesus College, Cambridge.

auburn hair, a strikingly handsome and distinguished figure. Miss Martineau wrote of him in her *Autobiography*:

A more simple - minded, virtuous man, full of domestic affections, than Mr. Malthus could not be found in all England. . . . Of all people in the world, Malthus was the one whom I heard quite easily without my trumpet;—Malthus, whose speech was hopelessly imperfect, from defect in the palate. I dreaded meeting him when invited by a friend of his who made my acquaintance on purpose. . . . When I considered my own deafness, and his inability to pronounce half the consonants, in the alphabet, and his hare-lip which must prevent my offering him my tube, I feared we should make a terrible business of it. I was delightfully wrong. His first sentence—slow and gentle with the vowels sonorous, whatever might become of the consonants—set me at ease completely. I soon found that the vowels are in fact all that I ever hear. His worst letter was *l*, and when I had no difficulty with his question,—"Would not you like to have a look at the lakes of Killarney?" I had nothing more to fear.

How this delightful scene brings us within reach of our own memories, separated by a gulf of aeons from Rousseau and Hume! Influenced too much by impressions of Dr. Johnson and Gibbon and Burke, we easily forget both the importance of the young radical England of the last quarter of the eighteenth century in which Malthus was brought up, and the destructive effect on it of the crushing disappointment of the outcome of the French Revolution (comparable to that which the outcome of the Russian Revolution may soon bring to their fellows of to-day)—though we know it in the evolution of Wordsworth and Coleridge and in the invincible ardour of Shelley—in making the passage from the eighteenth to the nineteenth century.   Malthus, at any rate, had now passed over completely in surroundings and intellectual outlook from the one century to the other.   Rousseau, his father Daniel, Gilbert Wakefield, the Cambridge of 1784, Paley, Pitt, the first edition of the *Essay* belonged to a different world and a different civilisation.   His links with ourselves grow close.   He was an original member of the Political Economy Club[1] which still dines on the first Wednesday of the month.[2]   He was also an original Fellow of the Royal Statistical Society, founded just before his death.   He attended the Cambridge meeting of the British Association in 1833.   Some readers of this essay may have known some of his pupils.

The most important influence of his later

[1] Mr. J. L. Mallet, in his diary of 1831, mentions that Malthus almost always attended the dinner.

[2] Before which I read, on April 2, 1924, an earlier version of this essay under the question, "What sort of man was the Reverend Robert Malthus?"

years was his intimacy with Ricardo, of whom he said:

I never loved anybody out of my own family so much. Our interchange of opinions was so unreserved, and the object after which we were both enquiring was so entirely the truth, and nothing else, that I cannot but think we sooner or later must have agreed.

As Maria Edgeworth, who knew both well, wrote of them:

They hunted together in search of Truth, and huzzaed when they found her, without caring who found her first; and indeed I have seen them both put their able hands to the windlass to drag her up from the bottom of that well in which she so strangely loves to dwell.

The friendship between Malthus and David Ricardo began in June 1811,[1] when Malthus "took the liberty of introducing himself" in the hope "that as we are *mainly* on the same side of the question, we might supersede the necessity of a long controversy in print respecting the points in which we differ, by an amicable discussion in private." It led to a long intimacy

---

[1] Mr. Sraffa tells me that this, and not February 1810 as given by Dr. Bonar, is the correct date. Mr. Sraffa's discovery of the Malthus side of the correspondence has enabled him to correct a wrong dating of certain letters ascribed by Dr. Bonar to 1810, but in fact belonging to 1813.

which was never broken. Ricardo paid repeated week-end visits to Haileybury; Malthus
seldom came to London without staying, or at
least breakfasting, with Ricardo, and in later
years was accustomed to stay with his family at
Gatcomb Park. It is evident that they had the
deepest affection and respect for one another.
The contrasts between the intellectual gifts of
the two were obvious and delightful. In
economic discussions Ricardo was the abstract
and *a priori* theorist, Malthus the inductive and
intuitive investigator who hated to stray too far
from what he could test by reference to the
facts and his own intuitions. But when it came
to practical finance, the rôles of the Jewish
stockbroker and the aristocratic clergyman were,
as they should be, reversed, as is illustrated by
a trifling incident which it is amusing to record.
During the Napoleonic War, Ricardo was, as
is well known, a principal member of a Syndicate which took part in operations in Government stocks corresponding to what is now
effected by "underwriting." His Syndicate
would take up by tender from the Treasury a
mixed bag of stocks of varying terms known as
the *Omnium*, which they would gradually dis-
pose of to the public as favourable opportunities
offered. On these occasions Ricardo was in
the habit of doing Malthus a friendly turn

by putting him down for a small participation without requiring him to put up any money,[1] which meant the certainty of a modest profit if Malthus did not hold on too long, since initially the Syndicate terms would always be comfortably below the current market price. Thus, as it happened, Malthus found himself a small "bull" of Government stock a few days before the battle of Waterloo. This was, unfortunately, too much for his nerves, and he instructed Ricardo, unless "it is either wrong or inconvenient to you," "to take an early opportunity of realising a small profit on the share you have been so good as to promise me." Ricardo carried out the instructions, though he himself by no means shared that view, since it appears that he carried over the week of Waterloo the maximum bull position of which his resources were capable. In a letter to Malthus of June 27, 1815, he modestly reports: "This is as great an advantage as ever I expect or wish to make by a rise. I have been a considerable gainer by the loan." "Now for a little of our old subject," he continues, and plunges back into the theory of the possible causes of a rise in the price of commodities.[2] Poor Malthus could not help being a little annoyed.

---

[1] Malthus speaks in one letter of taking about £5000 in the loan (Aug. 19, 1814).   [2] *Letters of Ricardo to Malthus*, p. 85.

I confess [he writes on July 16, 1815] I thought that the chances of the first battle were in favour of Buonaparte, who had the choice of attack; and it appears indeed from the Duke of Wellington's despatches that he was at one time very near succeeding. From what has happened since, however, it seems certain that the French were not so well prepared as they ought to have been. If there had been the energy and enthusiasm which might have been expected in the defence of their independence, one battle, however sanguinary and complete, could not have decided the fate of France.

This friendship will live in history on account of its having given rise to the most important literary correspondence in the whole development of Political Economy. In 1887 Dr. Bonar discovered Ricardo's side of the correspondence in the possession of Colonel Malthus, and published his well-known edition. But the search for Malthus's letters, which should have been in the possession of the Ricardo family, was made in vain. In 1907 Professor Foxwell published in the *Economic Journal* a single letter from the series, which David Ricardo happened to have given to Mrs. Smith of Easton Grey for her collection of autographs, and declared—with great prescience as it has turned out—that "the loss of Malthus's share in this correspondence may be ranked by economists next to that other literary disaster,

the destruction of David Hume's comments on
The Wealth of Nations."[1]   But Mr. Piero Sraffa,
from whom nothing is hid, has discovered the
missing letters in his researches for the forthcoming complete and definitive edition of the
Works of David Ricardo, which he is preparing
for the Royal Economic Society (to be published
in the course of the present year).   It will be
found that the publication of both sides of the
correspondence enhances its interest very greatly.
Here, indeed, are to be found the seeds of
economic theory, and also the divergent lines—
so divergent at the outset that the destination
can scarcely be recognised as the same until it
is reached—along which the subject can be
developed.   Ricardo is investigating the theory
of the *distribution* of the product in conditions
of equilibrium, and Malthus is concerned with
what determines the *volume* of output day by
day in the real world.   Malthus is dealing with
the monetary economy in which we happen to
live;   Ricardo with the abstraction of a neutral
money economy.[2]   They largely recognised the

[1] One other letter, having been sent by Ricardo to M'Culloch
and being with M'Culloch's papers in the British Museum, was
published by Prof. Hollander in 1895 in his Ricardo-M'Culloch
correspondence.

[2] For a good illustration of this *vide* Malthus's "Remarks on
Mr. Ricardo's Theory of Profits" in his *Principles of Political
Economy* (1st ed.), p. 326.

real source of their differences. In a letter of January 24, 1817, Ricardo wrote:

It appears to me that one great cause of our difference in opinion on the subjects which we have so often discussed is that you have always in your mind the immediate and temporary effects of particular changes, whereas I put these immediate and temporary effects quite aside, and fix my whole attention on the permanent state of things which will result from them. Perhaps you estimate these temporary effects too highly, whilst I am too much disposed to undervalue them. To manage the subject quite right, they should be carefully distinguished and mentioned, and the due effects ascribed to each.

To which Malthus replied with considerable effect on January 26, 1817:

I agree with you that one cause of our difference in opinion is that which you mention. I certainly am disposed to refer frequently to things as they are, as the only way of making one's writings practically useful to society, and I think also the only way of being secure from falling into the errors of the taylors of Laputa, and by a slight mistake at the outset arrive at conclusions the most distant from the truth. Besides I really think that the progress of society consists of irregular movements, and that to omit the consideration of causes which for eight or ten years will give a great *stimulus* to production and population, or a great *check* to them, is to omit the causes of the wealth and poverty of nations—the grand object of all enquiries in Political Economy. A writer may, to be sure, make any hypothesis he pleases; but if he supposes what is not at all true practically, he precludes himself from drawing any practical inferences from his hypotheses. In your essay on profits you suppose the real wages of labour constant; but as they vary with every alteration in the prices of commodities (while they remain nominally the same) and are in reality as variable as profits, there is no chance of your inferences being just as applied to the actual state of things.[1] We see in all the countries around us, and in our own particularly, periods of greater and less prosperity and sometimes of adversity, but *never* the uniform progress which you seem alone to contemplate.

But to come to a still more specific and fundamental cause of our difference, I think it is this. You seem to think that the wants and tastes of mankind are always ready for the supply; while I am most decidedly of opinion that few things are more difficult than to inspire new tastes and wants, particularly out of old materials; that one of the great elements of demand is the value that people set upon commodities, and that the more completely the supply is suited to the demand the higher will this value be, and the more days' labour will it exchange for, or give the power of commanding. . . . I am quite of opinion that *practically* the actual check to produce and population arises more from want of stimulus than want of power to produce.

One cannot rise from a perusal of this correspondence without a feeling that the almost

---

[1] This point is further developed in the "Remarks on Mr. Ricardo's Theory of Profits" referred to in the footnote above.

total obliteration of Malthus's line of approach and the complete domination of Ricardo's for a period of a hundred years has been a disaster to the progress of economics. Time after time in these letters Malthus is talking plain sense, the force of which Ricardo with his head in the clouds wholly fails to comprehend. Time after time a crushing refutation by Malthus is met by a mind so completely closed that Ricardo does not even see what Malthus is saying. I must not, however, further anticipate the importance of the forthcoming publication of Mr. Piero Sraffa, to whose generosity I owe the opportunity of making these excerpts, except to show Malthus's complete comprehension of the effects of excessive saving on output *via* its effects on profit.

As early as October 9, 1814, in the letter printed by Prof. Foxwell in the *Economic Journal* (1907, p. 274), Malthus was writing:

I cannot by any means agree with you in your observation that "the desire of accumulation will occasion demand just as *effectually* as a desire to consume" and that "consumption and accumulation equally promote demand." I confess indeed that I know no other cause for the fall of profits which I believe you will allow generally takes place from accumulation than that the price of produce falls compared with the expense of production, or in other words that the *effective* demand is diminished.

But the following extracts from two letters written by Malthus in July 1821 show that by that date the matter was still clearer in his mind and foggier still in Ricardo's:

[July 7, 1821]

We see in almost every part of the world vast powers of production which are not put into action, and I explain this phenomenon by saying that from the want of a proper distribution of the actual produce adequate motives are not furnished to continued production. By inquiring into the immediate causes of the progress of wealth, I clearly mean to inquire mainly into motives. I don't at all wish to deny that some persons or others are entitled to consume all that is produced; but the grand question is whether it is distributed in such a manner between the different parties concerned as to occasion the most effective demand for future produce: and I distinctly maintain that an attempt to accumulate very rapidly which necessarily implies a considerable diminution of unproductive consumption, by greatly impairing the usual motives to production must prematurely check the progress of wealth. This surely is the great *practical* question, and not whether we ought to call the sort of stagnation which would be thus occasioned a glut. That I hold to be a matter of very subordinate importance. But if it be true that an attempt to accumulate very rapidly will occasion such a division between labour and profits as almost to destroy both the motive and the power of future accumulation and consequently the power of maintaining and employing an increasing population, must

it not be acknowledged that such an attempt to accumulate, or that saving too much, may be really prejudicial
to a country.

[July 16, 1821]

With regard to our present subject of discussion, it
seems as if we should never thoroughly understand each
other, and I almost despair of being ever able to explain
myself, if you could read the two first paragraphs of
the first section of my last chapter, and yet "understand
me to say that vast powers of production are put into
action, and the result is unfavourable to the interests
of mankind." I expressly say that it is my object to
show what are the causes which call forth the powers
of production; and if I recommend a certain proportion
of unproductive consumption, it is obviously and expressly with the sole view of furnishing the necessary
motive to the greatest continued production. And I
think still that this certain proportion of unproductive
consumption varying according to the fertility of the
soil, etc., is absolutely and indispensably necessary to
call forth the resources of a country. . . . Now among
the motives to produce, one of the most essential certainly is that an adequate share of what is produced
should belong to those who set all industry in motion.
But you yourself allow that a great temporary saving,
commencing when profits were sufficient to encourage
it, might occasion such a division of the produce as
would leave no motive to a further increase of production. And if a state of things in which for a time
there is no motive to a further increase of production
be not properly denominated a stagnation, I do not
know what can be so called; particularly as this

stagnation must inevitably throw the rising generation out of employment. We know from repeated experience that the money price of labour never falls till many workmen have been for some time out of work. And the question is, whether this stagnation of capital, and subsequent stagnation in the demand for labour arising from increased production without an adequate proportion of unproductive consumption on the part of the landlords and capitalists, could take place without prejudice to the country, without occasioning a less degree both of happiness and wealth than would have occurred if the unproductive consumption of the landlords and capitalists had been so proportioned to the natural surplus of the society as to have continued uninterrupted the motives to production, and prevented first an unnatural demand for labour, and then a necessary and sudden diminution of such demand. But if this be so, how can it be said with truth that parsimony, though it may be prejudicial to the producers cannot be prejudicial to the state; or that an increase of unproductive consumption among landlords and capitalists may not sometimes be the proper remedy for a state of things in which the motives to production fail.

If only Malthus, instead of Ricardo, had been the parent stem from which nineteenth-century economics proceeded, what a much wiser and richer place the world would be to-day! We have laboriously to re-discover and force through the obscuring envelopes of our misguided education what should never have ceased to be obvious. I have long claimed

Robert Malthus as the first of the Cambridge economists; and we can do so, after the publication of these letters, with increased sympathy and admiration.

In these letters Malthus was indeed only re-stating from his *Principles of Political Economy*, published in 1820, the argument of Chapter VII. Section IX. "Of the Distribution occasioned by unproductive consumers, considered as a Means of increasing the exchangeable Value of the whole Produce," which had wholly failed to enter the comprehension of Ricardo just as it has failed to influence the ideas of posterity. But he makes it much clearer. If we go back, however, to the *Political Economy* with our attention awakened, it is evident that the essence of the argument is there set forth.[1]   In Section X. of the same chapter Malthus proceeded to apply these principles "to the Distresses of the Labouring Classes since 1815." He points out that the trouble was due to the diversion of re-sources, previously devoted to war, to the accumulation of savings; that in such circum-stances deficiency of savings could not possibly be the cause, and saving, though a private virtue, had ceased to be a public duty; and that public

[1] I refer the reader to the whole of Section IX. as a masterly exposition of the conditions which determine the *optimum* of Saving in the actual economic system in which we live.

L

works and expenditure by landlords and persons of property was the appropriate remedy. The two passages following may be quoted as illustrations from the best economic analysis ever written of the events of 1815–20:

When profits are low and uncertain, when capitalists are quite at a loss where they can safely employ their capitals, and when on these accounts capital is flowing out of the country; in short, when all the evidence which the nature of the subject admits, distinctly proves that there is no effective demand for capital at home, is it not contrary to the general principles of political economy, is it not a vain and fruitless opposition to that first, greatest, and most universal of all its principles, the principle of supply and demand, to recommend saving, and the conversion of more revenue into capital? Is it not just the same sort of thing as to recommend marriage when people are starving and emigrating? [1]

Altogether I should say, that the employment of the poor in roads and public works, and a tendency among landlords and persons of property to build, to improve and beautify their grounds, and to employ workmen and menial servants, are the means most within our power and most directly calculated to remedy the evils arising from that disturbance in the balance of produce and consumption, which has been occasioned by the sudden conversion of soldiers, sailors, and various other classes which the war employed, into productive labourers. [2]

The whole problem of the balance between

[1] *Op. cit.* (1st ed.) p. 495.   [2] *Op. cit.* p. 512.

Saving and Investment had been posed in the *Preface* to the book, as follows:

Adam Smith has stated, that capitals are increased by parsimony, that every frugal man is a public benefactor, and that the increase of wealth depends upon the balance of produce above consumption. That these propositions are true to a great extent is perfectly unquestionable. . . . But it is quite obvious that they are not true to an indefinite extent, and that the principles of saving, pushed to excess, would destroy the motive to production. If every person were satisfied with the simplest food, the poorest clothing, and the meanest houses, it is certain that no other sort of food, clothing, and lodging would be in existence. . . . The two extremes are obvious; and it follows that there must be some intermediate point, though the resources of political economy may not be able to ascertain it, where, taking into consideration both the power to produce and the will to consume, the encouragement to the increase of wealth is the greatest.[1]

Surely it was a great fault in Ricardo to fail entirely to see any significance in this line of thought. But Malthus's defect lay in his overlooking entirely the part played by the rate of interest. Twenty years ago I should have retorted to Malthus that the state of affairs he envisages could not occur unless the rate of interest had first fallen to zero. Malthus perceived, as often, what was true; but it is essential

[1] *Op. cit.* pp. 8, 9.

to a complete comprehension of why it is true,
to explain how an excess of frugality does not
bring with it a decline to zero in the rate of
interest.

Adam Smith and Malthus and Ricardo!
There is something about these three figures
to evoke more than ordinary sentiments from
us their children in the spirit. Malthus and
Ricardo were not hindered by the contrary
qualities of their minds from conversing together in peace and amity all their days. The
last sentence in Ricardo's last letter to Malthus
before his death runs:

And now, my dear Malthus, I have done. Like
other disputants, after much discussion, we each retain
our own opinions. These discussions, however, never
influence our friendship; I should not like you more
than I do if you agreed in opinion with me.

Malthus survived his friend by ten years, and
then he too had done.

My views are before the public [he wrote shortly
before his death]. If I am to alter anything, I can do
little more than alter the language: and I don't know
that I should alter it for the better.

In 1833, the year before his death, Miss
Martineau visited him at Haileybury. She was
pleased with "the well-planted county of Herts.
Almost daily we went forth when work was

done—a pleasant riding party of five or six, and explored all the green lanes, and enjoyed all the fine views in the neighbourhood. The families of the other professors made up a very pleasant society—to say nothing of the interest of seeing in the students the future administrators of India. The subdued jests and external homage and occasional insurrections of the young men; the archery of the young ladies; the curious politeness of the Persian professor; the fine learning and eager scholarship of Principal Le Bas, and the somewhat old-fashioned courtesies of the summer evening parties are all over now."

ALFRED MARSHALL [1]

I

ALFRED MARSHALL was born at Clapham on
July 26, 1842, the son of William Marshall, a
cashier in the Bank of England, by his marriage
with Rebecca Oliver. The Marshalls were a
clerical family of the West, sprung from William
Marshall, incumbent of Saltash, Cornwall, at
the end of the seventeenth century. Alfred
was the great-great-grandson of the Reverend
William Marshall, [2] the half-legendary herculean
parson of Devonshire, who, by twisting horse-

[1] In the preparation of this Memoir (August 1924) I had
great assistance from Mrs. Marshall. I have to thank her for
placing at my disposal a number of papers and for writing out
some personal notes from which I have quoted freely. Alfred
Marshall himself left in writing several autobiographical scraps,
of which I have made the best use I could. I prepared in 1924
a complete bibliographical list of the writings of Alfred Marshall,
which was printed in the *Economic Journal,* December 1926, and
reprinted in *Memorials of Alfred Marshall* (edited by A. C. Pigou,
1925).

[2] By his third wife, Mary Kitson, the first child he christened
in his parish, of whom he said in joke that she should be his little
wife, as she duly was twenty years later.

[Photo. Elliott & Fry

ALFRED MARSHALL

1892

shoes with his hands, frightened local black-
smiths into fearing that they blew their bellows
for the devil.[1] His great-grandfather was the
Reverend John Marshall, Headmaster of Exeter
Grammar School, who married Mary Hawtrey,
daughter of the Reverend Charles Hawtrey,
Sub-Dean and Canon of Exeter, and aunt of the
Provost of Eton.[2]

His father, the cashier in the Bank of England, was a tough old character, of great resolution and perception, cast in the mould of the
strictest Evangelicals, bony neck, bristly pro-
jecting chin, author of an Evangelical epic in a
sort of Anglo-Saxon language of his own invention which found some favour in its appropriate
circles, surviving despotically minded into his
ninety-second year. The nearest objects of his
masterful instincts were his family, and their
easiest victim his wife; but their empire ex-

[1] This is one of many stories of his prodigious strength which
A. M. was fond of telling—how, for example, driving a pony-
trap in a narrow Devonshire lane and meeting another vehicle, he
took the pony out and lifted the trap clean over the hedge. But
we come to something more prognostical of Alfred in a little
device of William Marshall's latter days. Being in old age heavy
and unwieldy, yet so affected with gout as to be unable to walk
up and down stairs, he had a hole made in the ceiling of the room
in which he usually sat, through which he was drawn in his chair
by pulleys to and from his bedroom above.

[2] Thus Alfred Marshall was third cousin once removed to
Ralph Hawtrey, author of *Currency and Credit*. A. M. drew
more from the subtle Hawtreys than from the Reverend Hercules.

tended in theory over the whole of womankind, the old gentleman writing a tract entitled *Man's Rights and Woman's Duties*. Heredity is mighty, and Alfred Marshall did not altogether escape the influence of the parental mould. An implanted masterfulness towards womankind warred in him with the deep affection and admiration which he bore to his own wife, and with an environment which threw him in closest touch with the education and liberation of women.

II

At nine years of age Alfred was sent to Merchant Taylors' School, for which his father, perceiving the child's ability, had begged a nomination from a Director of the Bank.[1] In mingled affection and severity his father recalls James Mill. He used to make the boy work with him for school, often at Hebrew, until eleven at night. Indeed, Alfred was so much overworked by his father that, he used to say, his life was saved by his Aunt Louisa, with whom he spent long summer holidays near Dawlish. She gave him a boat and a gun and a pony, and by the end of the summer he would return home, brown and well. E. C. Dermer,

---

[1] "Do you know that you are asking me for £200?" said the Director; but he gave it.

his fellow-monitor at Merchant Taylors', tells that at school he was small and pale, badly dressed, looked overworked, and was called "tallow candles"; that he cared little for games, was fond of propounding chess problems,[1] and did not readily make friends.[2]

Rising to be Third Monitor, he became entitled in 1861, under old statutes, to a scholarship at St. John's College, Oxford, which would have led in three years to a Fellowship, and would have furnished him with the same permanence of security as belonged in those days to Eton scholars at King's or Winchester scholars at New College. It was the first step to ordination in the Evangelical ministry for which his father designed him. But this was

[1] Mrs. Marshall writes: "As a boy, Alfred suffered severely from headache, for which the only cure was to play chess. His father therefore allowed chess for this purpose; but later on he made A. promise never to play chess. This promise was kept all through his life, though he could never see a chess problem in the newspapers without getting excited. But he said that his father was right to exact this promise, for otherwise he would have been tempted to spend all his time on it." A. M. himself once said: "We are not at liberty to play chess games, or exercise ourselves upon subtleties that lead nowhere. It is well for the young to enjoy the mere pleasure of action, physical or intellectual. But the time presses; the responsibility on us is heavy."

[2] His chief school friends were H. D. Traill, later Fellow of St. John's College, Oxford, and Sidney Hall, afterwards an artist. Traill's brother gave him a copy of Mill's *Logic*, which Traill and he read with enthusiasm and discussed at meals at the Monitors' table.

not the main point for Alfred—it meant a continued servitude to the Classics.[1] He had painful recollections in later days of his tyrant father keeping him awake into the night for the better study of Hebrew, whilst at the same time forbidding him the fascinating paths of mathematics. His father hated the sight of a mathematical book, but Alfred would conceal Potts' Euclid in his pocket as he walked to and from school. He read a proposition and then worked it out in his mind as he walked along, standing still at intervals, with his toes turned in. The fact that the curriculum of the Sixth Form at Merchant Taylors' reached so far as the differential calculus had excited native proclivities. Airy, the mathematical master, said that "he had a genius for mathematics." Mathematics

---

[1] Near the end of his life A. M. wrote the following characteristic sentences about his classical studies: "When at school I was told to take no account of accents in pronouncing Greek words, I concluded that to burden my memory with accents would take up time and energy that might be turned to account; so I did not look out my accents in the dictionary; and received the only very heavy punishment of my life. This suggested to me that classical studies do not induce an appreciation of the value of time; and I turned away from them as far as I could towards mathematics. In later years I have observed that fine students of science are greedy of time: but many classical men seem to value it lightly. I will add that my headmaster was a broad-minded man; and succeeded in making his head form write Latin Essays, thought out in Latin: not thought out in English and translated into Latin. I am more grateful for that than for anything else he did for me."

represented for Alfred emancipation, and he used to rejoice greatly that his father could not understand them. No! he would not be buried at Oxford under dead languages; he would run away—to be a cabin-boy at Cambridge and climb the rigging of geometry and spy out the heavens.

At this point there comes on the scene a well-disposed uncle, willing to lend him a little money (for his father was too poor to help further when the Oxford Scholarship was abandoned)—repaid by Alfred soon after taking his degree from what he earned by teaching—which, with a Parkin's Exhibition[1] of £40 a year from St. John's College, Cambridge,[2] opened to him the doors of Mathematics and of Cambridge. Since it was a legacy of £250 from this same uncle which enabled him, fourteen years later, to pay his visit to the United States, the story of the sources of this uncle's wealth, which Alfred often told, deserve a record here. Having sought his fortunes in Australia

[1] He was promoted to a Scholarship in the same year.

[2] There is a letter from Dr. Bateson, Master of St. John's, to Dr. Hessey, Headmaster of Merchant Taylors', dated June 15, 1861, announcing this Exhibition, and giving early evidence of the interest which Dr. Bateson—like Dr. Jowett in later days—always maintained in Alfred Marshall. When A. M. applied for the Bristol appointment in 1877, Dr. Bateson wrote: "I have a great admiration for his character, which is remarkable for its great simplicity, earnestness, and self-sacrificing conscientiousness."

and being established there at the date of the gold discoveries, a little family eccentricity disposed him to seek his benefit indirectly. So he remained a pastoralist, but, to the mirth of his neighbours, refused to employ anyone about his place who did not suffer from some physical defect, staffing himself entirely with the halt, the blind, and the maimed. When the gold boom reached its height his reward came. All the able-bodied labourers migrated to the goldfields and Charles Marshall was the only man in the place able to carry on. A few years later he returned to England with a fortune, ready to take an interest in a clever, rebellious nephew.

In 1917 Marshall put into writing the following account of his methods of work at this time and later:

An epoch in my life occurred when I was, I think, about seventeen years old. I was in Regent Street, and saw a workman standing idle before a shop-window: but his face indicated alert energy, so I stood still and watched. He was preparing to sketch on the window of a shop guiding lines for a short statement of the business concerned, which was to be shown by white letters fixed to the glass. Each stroke of arm and hand needed to be made with a single free sweep, so as to give a graceful result; it occupied perhaps two seconds of keen excitement. He stayed still for a few minutes after each stroke, so that his pulse might grow quiet. If he had saved the ten minutes thus lost, his employers would have been injured by more than the value of his wages for a whole day. That set up a train of thought which led me to the resolve never to use my mind when it was not fresh, and to regard the intervals between successive strains as sacred to absolute repose. When I went to Cambridge and became full master of myself, I resolved never to read a mathematical book for more than a quarter of an hour at a time without a break. I had some light literature always by my side, and in the breaks I read through more than once nearly the whole of Shakespeare, Boswell's *Life of Johnson*, the *Agamemnon* of Æschylus (the only Greek play which I could read without effort), a great part of Lucretius and so on. Of course I often got excited by my mathematics, and read for half an hour or more without stopping: but that meant that my mind was intense, and no harm was done.

A power of intense concentration for brief periods, combined with a lack of power of continuous concentration, was characteristic of him all his life. He was seldom able to execute at white heat any considerable piece of work. He was also bothered by the lack of a retentive memory: even as an undergraduate his mathematical book-work troubled him as much as the problems did. As a boy he had a strong arithmetical faculty, which he afterwards lost.

Meanwhile at St. John's College, Cambridge, Alfred Marshall fulfilled his ambitions. In

1865 he was Second Wrangler,[1] the year when
Lord Rayleigh was Senior, and he was immediately elected to a Fellowship.   He proposed to
devote himself to the study of molecular physics.
Meanwhile he earned his living (and repaid
Uncle Charles) by becoming for a brief period
a mathematical master at Clifton, under Percival,
for whom he had a great veneration.   A little
later he returned to Cambridge and took up
coaching for the Mathematical Tripos for a
short time.   In this way "Mathematics," he
said, "had paid my arrears.   I was free for my
own inclinations."

The main importance of Marshall's time at
Clifton was that he made friends with H. G.
Dakyns, who had gone there as an assistant
master on the foundation of Clifton College in
1862, and, through him, with J. R. Mozley.
These friendships opened to him the door into
the intellectual circle of which Henry Sidgwick
was the centre.   Up to this time there is no
evidence of Marshall's having been in touch
with the more eminent of his contemporaries,
but soon after his return to Cambridge he
became a member of the small informal Discussion Society known as the "Grote Club."

The Grote Club came into existence with

---

[1] One of the famous band of Second Wranglers, which includes
Whewell, Clerk Maxwell, Kelvin, and W. K. Clifford.

discussions after dinner in the Trumpington
Vicarage of the Reverend John Grote, who was
Knightbridge Professor of Moral Philosophy
from 1855 till his death in 1866. The original
members, besides Grote, were Henry Sidgwick,
Aldis Wright, J. B. Mayor, and John Venn.[1]
J. R. Mozley of King's and J. B. Pearson of St.
John's joined a little later. Marshall wrote[2]
the following account of his own connection
with the Society:

When I was admitted in 1867, the active members
were Professor F. D. Maurice (Grote's successor), Sidgwick, Venn, J. R. Mozley and J. B. Pearson. . . .
After 1867 or 1868 the club languished a little; but
new vigour was soon imparted to it by the advent of
W. K. Clifford and J. F. Moulton. For a year or two
Sidgwick, Mozley, Clifford, Moulton, and myself were
the active members; and we all attended regularly.
Clifford and Moulton had at that time read but little
philosophy; so they kept quiet for the first half-hour
of the discussion, and listened eagerly to what others,
and especially Sidgwick, said. Then they let their
tongues loose, and the pace was tremendous. If I might
have verbatim reports of a dozen of the best conversa-
tions I have heard, I should choose two or three from
among those evenings in which Sidgwick and Clifford
were the chief speakers. Another would certainly be
a conversation at tea before a Grote Club meeting, of

[1] For Dr. Venn's account of early meetings see *Henry Sidgwick:
a Memoir*, p. 134.
[2] Printed in *Henry Sidgwick: a Memoir*, p. 137.

which I have unfortunately no record (I think it was early in 1868), in which practically no one spoke but Maurice and Sidgwick. Sidgwick devoted himself to drawing out Maurice's recollections of English social and political life in the thirties, forties, and fifties. Maurice's face shone out bright, with its singular holy radiance, as he responded to Sidgwick's inquiries and suggestions; and we others said afterwards that we owed all the delight of that evening to him. . . .

It was at this time and under these influences that there came the crisis in his mental development of which in later years he often spoke. His design to study physics was (in his own words) "cut short by the sudden rise of a deep interest in the philosophical foundation of knowledge, especially in relation to theology."

In Marshall's undergraduate days at Cambridge a preference for Mathematics over Classics had not interfered with the integrity of his early religious beliefs. He still looked forward to ordination, and his zeal directed itself at times towards the field of Foreign Missions. A missionary he remained all his life, but after a quick struggle religious beliefs dropped away and he became, for the rest of his life, what used to be called an agnostic. Of his relationship to Sidgwick at this time, Marshall spoke as follows (at the meeting for a Sidgwick Memorial, Trinity Lodge, November 26, 1900):

Though not his pupil in name, I was in substance his pupil in Moral Science, and I am the oldest of them in residence. I was fashioned by him. He was, so to speak, my spiritual father and mother: for I went to him for aid when perplexed, and for comfort when troubled; and I never returned empty away. The minutes that I spent with him were not ordinary minutes; they helped me to live. I had to pass through troubles and doubts somewhat similar to those with which he, with broader knowledge and greater strength, had fought his way; and perhaps of all the people who have cause to be grateful to him, none has more than I.

Marshall's Cambridge career came just at the date which will, I think, be regarded by the historians of opinion as the critical moment at which Christian dogma fell away from the serious philosophical world of England, or at any rate of Cambridge. In 1863 Henry Sidgwick, aged twenty-four, had subscribed to the Thirty-Nine Articles as a condition of tenure of his Fellowship,[1] and was occupied in reading Deuteronomy in Hebrew and preparing lectures on the Acts of the Apostles. Mill, the greatest intellectual influence on the youth of the age, had written nothing which clearly indicated any divergence from received religious opinions up to his *Examination of Hamilton* in 1865.[2] At

[1] He had decided in 1861 not to take orders.

[2] Mill's *Essays on Religion*, which gave his final opinions, were not published until 1874, after his death.

M

about this time Leslie Stephen was an Anglican clergyman, James Ward a Nonconformist minister, Alfred Marshall a candidate for holy orders, W. K. Clifford a High Churchman. In 1869 Sidgwick resigned his Trinity Fellowship, "to free myself from dogmatic obligations." A little later none of these could have been called Christians. Nevertheless, Marshall, like Sidgwick,[1] was as far as possible from adopting an "anti-religious" attitude. He sympathised with Christian morals and Christian ideals and Christian incentives. There is nothing in his writings depreciating religion in any form; few of his pupils could have spoken definitely about his religious opinions. At the end of his life he said, "Religion seems to me an attitude," and that, though he had given up Theology, he believed more and more in Religion.

The great change-over of the later sixties was an intellectual change, not the ethical or emotional change which belongs to a later generation, and it was a wholly intellectual debate which brought it about. Marshall was wont to attribute the beginning of his own transition of mind to the controversy arising out of H. L. Mansel's *Bampton Lectures*, which was first put

---

[1] For a most interesting summary of Sidgwick's attitude in later life, see his *Memoir*, p. 505. Or see the last paragraph of W. K. Clifford's "Ethics of Religion" (*Lectures and Essays*, ii. 244) for another characteristic reaction of Marshall's generation.

into his hands by J. R. Mozley. Mansel means nothing to the present generation. But, as the protagonist of the last attempt to found Christian dogma on an intellectual basis, he was of the greatest importance in the sixties. In 1858, Mansel, an Oxford don and afterwards Dean of St. Paul's, "adopted from Hamilton [1] the peculiar theory which was to enlist Kant in the service of the Church of England" [2]—an odd tergiversation of the human mind, the influence of which was great in Oxford for a full fifty years. Mansel's *Bampton Lectures* of 1858 brought him to the front as an intellectual champion of orthodoxy. In 1865, the year in which Marshall took his degree and had begun to turn his mind to the four quarters of heaven, there appeared Mill's *Examination of Sir William Hamilton's Philosophy*, which included a criticism of Mansel's extension of Hamilton to Christian Theology. Mansel replied. Mansel's defence of orthodoxy "showed me," Marshall said, "how much there was to be defended." The great controversy dominated Marshall's thoughts and

[1] In 1836 Sir William Hamilton, having established his genealogy and made good his claim to a baronetcy, had been appointed to the Chair of Logic and Metaphysics at Edinburgh, and delivered during the next eight years the famous lectures which attempted the dangerous task of superimposing influences drawn from Kant and the German philosophers on the Scottish tradition of common sense.

[2] Stephen, *English Utilitarians*, iii. 382.

drove him for a time to metaphysical studies, and then onward to the social sciences.

Meanwhile in 1859, the year following the *Bampton Lectures*, the *Origin of Species* had appeared, to point away from heaven or the clouds to an open road on earth; and in 1860–1862 Herbert Spencer's *First Principles* (unreadable as it now is), also born out of the Hamilton-Mansel controversy, took a new direction, dissolved metaphysics in agnosticism, and warned all but ingrained metaphysical minds away from a blind alley. Metaphysical agnosticism, Evolutionary progress, and—the one remnant still left of the intellectual inheritance of the previous generation—Utilitarian ethics joined to propel the youthful mind in a new direction.

From Metaphysics, therefore, Marshall turned his mind to Ethics. It would be true, I suppose, to say that Marshall never departed explicitly from the Utilitarian ideas which dominated the generation of economists which preceded him. But it is remarkable with what caution—in which respect he goes far beyond Sidgwick and is at the opposite pole from Jevons —he handled all such matters. There is, I think, no passage in his works in which he links economic studies to any ethical doctrine in particular. The solution of economic problems was for Marshall not an application of the hedonistic calculus, but a prior condition of the exercise of man's higher faculties, irrespective, almost, of what we mean by "higher." The economist can claim, and this claim is sufficient for his purposes, that "the study of the causes of poverty is the study of the causes of the degradation of a large part of mankind." [1] Correspondingly, the possibility of progress "depends in a great measure upon facts and inferences, which are within the province of economics; and this it is which gives to economic studies their chief and their highest interest." [2] This remains true even though the question also "depends partly on the moral and political capabilities of human nature; and on these matters the economist has no special means of information; he must do as others do, and guess as best he can." [3]

This was his final position. Nevertheless, it was only through Ethics that he first reached Economics. In a retrospect of his mental history, drawn from him towards the end of his life, he said:

From Metaphysics I went to Ethics, and thought that the justification of the existing condition of society was not easy. A friend, who had read a great deal of

---

[1] *Principles* (1st ed.), pp. 3, 4.
[2] *Ibid.*   [3] *Ibid.*

what are now called the Moral Sciences, constantly said: "Ah! if you understood Political Economy you would not say that." So I read Mill's *Political Economy* and got much excited about it. I had doubts as to the propriety of inequalities of *opportunity*, rather than of material comfort. Then, in my vacations I visited the poorest quarters of several cities and walked through one street after another, looking at the faces of the poorest people. Next, I resolved to make as thorough a study as I could of Political Economy.

His passage into Economics is also described in his own words in some pages,[1] written about 1917 and designed for the Preface to *Money, Credit and Commerce*:

About the year 1867 (while mainly occupied with teaching Mathematics at Cambridge), Mansel's *Bampton Lectures* came into my hands and caused me to think that man's own possibilities were the most important subject for his study. So I gave myself for a time to the study of Metaphysics; but soon passed to what seemed to be the more progressive study of Psychology. Its fascinating inquiries into the possibilities of the higher and more rapid development of human faculties brought me into touch with the question: how far do the conditions of life of the British (and other) working classes

[1] Rescued by Mrs. Marshall from the waste-paper basket, whither too great a proportion of the results of his mental toil found their way; like his great-great-uncle, the Reverend Richard Marshall, who is said to have been a good poet and was much pressed to publish his compositions, to which, however, he had so great an objection that lest it be done after his death he burnt all his papers.

generally suffice for fullness of life? Older and wiser men told me that the resources of production do not suffice for affording to the great body of the people the leisure and the opportunity for study; and they told me that I needed to study Political Economy. I followed their advice, and regarded myself as a wanderer in the land of dry facts; looking forward to a speedy return to the luxuriance of pure thought. But the more I studied economic science, the smaller appeared the knowledge which I had of it, in proportion to the knowledge that I needed; and now, at the end of nearly half a century of almost exclusive study of it, I am conscious of more ignorance of it than I was at the beginning of the study.

In 1868, when he was still in his metaphysical stage, a desire to read Kant in the original led him to Germany. "Kant my guide," he once said, "the only man I ever worshipped: but I could not get further: beyond seemed misty, and social problems came imperceptibly to the front. Are the opportunities of real life to be confined to a few?" He lived at Dresden with a German professor who had previously coached Henry Sidgwick.[1] Hegel's *Philosophy of History* greatly influenced him. He also came in contact with the work of the German economists, particularly Roscher. Finally Dr. Bateson, the Master of St. John's, was instrumental in giving him a career in life

---

[1] He was again in Germany, living in Berlin, in the winter of 1870–71, during the Franco-German War.

by persuading the College to establish for him a special lectureship in Moral Science.[1]　He soon settled down to Economics, though for a time he gave short courses on other branches of Moral Science—on Logic and on Bentham.[2]

His dedication to economic study—for so he always considered it, not less ordained in spirit than if he had fulfilled his father's desire—was now effected.　His two years of doubt and disturbance of mind left on his imagination a deep impression, to which in later years he would often recur with pupils whom he deemed worthy of the high calling—for so he reckoned it—of studying with scientific disinterestedness the modes and principles of the daily business of life, by which human happiness and the opportunities for good life are, in great measure, determined.

[1] In a conversation I had with him a few weeks before his death he dwelt especially on Hegel's *Philosophy of History* and the friendly action of Dr. Bateson as finally determining the course of his life. Since J. B. Mayor, the first "Moral Science lecturer" in Cambridge, had held a similar lectureship at St. John's for some time, whilst the Rev. J. B. Pearson was also a Johnian and a moral scientist, the appointment of another lecturer in the subject was a somewhat unusual step.　Henry Sidgwick had been appointed to a lectureship in Moral Science at Trinity in the previous year, 1867; and Venn had come back to Cambridge as a Moral Science lecturer at Caius in 1862.

[2] Mrs. Marshall remembers how in the early seventies at Newnham, Mary Kennedy (Mrs. R. T. Wright) and she had to write for him "a dialogue between Bentham and an Ascetic."

Before we leave the early phase, when he was not yet an economist, we may pause a moment to consider the colour of his outlook on life as, at that time, it was already fixed in him.

Like his two colleagues, Henry Sidgwick and James Ward, in the Chairs of the Moral Sciences at Cambridge during the last decades of the nineteenth century, Alfred Marshall belonged to the tribe of sages and pastors; yet, like them also, endowed with a double nature, he was a scientist too. As a preacher and pastor of men he was not particularly superior to other similar natures. As a scientist he was, within his own field, the greatest in the world for a hundred years. Nevertheless, it was to the first side of his nature that he himself preferred to give the pre-eminence. This self should be master, he thought; the second self, servant. The second self sought knowledge for its own sake; the first self subordinated abstract aims to the need for practical advancement. The piercing eyes and ranging wings of an eagle were often called back to earth to do the bidding of a moraliser.

This double nature was the clue to Marshall's mingled strength and weakness; to his own conflicting purposes and waste of strength; to the two views which could always be taken about him; to the sympathies and antipathies he inspired.

In another respect the diversity of his nature was pure advantage. The study of economics does not seem to require any specialised gifts of an unusually high order. Is it not, intellectually regarded, a very easy subject compared with the higher branches of philosophy and pure science? Yet good, or even competent, economists are the rarest of birds. An easy subject, at which very few excel! The paradox finds its explanation, perhaps, in that the master-economist must possess a rare *combination* of gifts. He must reach a high standard in several different directions and must combine talents not often found together. He must be mathematician, historian, statesman, philosopher—in some degree. He must understand symbols and speak in words. He must contemplate the particular in terms of the general, and touch abstract and concrete in the same flight of thought. He must study the present in the light of the past for the purposes of the future. No part of man's nature or his institutions must lie entirely outside his regard. He must be purposeful and disinterested in a simultaneous mood; as aloof and incorruptible as an artist, yet sometimes as near the earth as a politician. Much, but not all, of this ideal many-sidedness Marshall possessed. But chiefly his mixed training and divided nature furnished him with the most essential and fundamental of the economist's necessary gifts—he was conspicuously historian and mathematician, a dealer in the particular and the general, the temporal and the eternal, at the same time.

III

The task of expounding the development of Marshall's Economics is rendered difficult by the long intervals which generally separated the initial discovery and its oral communication to pupils from the final publication in a book to the world outside. Before attempting this it will be convenient to trace briefly the outward course of his life from his appointment to a lectureship at St. John's College, Cambridge, in 1868 to his succession to the Chair of Political Economy in Cambridge in 1885.

For nine years Marshall remained Fellow and Lecturer of St. John's, laying the foundations of his subject but publishing nothing.[1] After his introduction to the Grote Club he was particularly intimate with W. K. Clifford[2] and

[1] The occasional articles belonging to this period are included in a Bibliography which I printed in the *Economic Journal*, December 1924.

[2] Clifford, who was three years Marshall's junior, came up to Trinity in 1863, was elected to a Fellowship in 1868, and resided in Cambridge, where his rooms were "the meeting point of a numerous body of friends" (*vide* Sir F. Pollock's Memoir), until 1871.

Fletcher Moulton.   Clifford was chief favourite, though "he was too fond of astonishing
people."   As a member, a little later on, of the
"Eranus" he was in touch with Sidgwick, Venn,
Fawcett, Henry Jackson, and other leaders of
that first age of the emancipation of Cambridge.
At this time he used to go abroad almost every
long vacation.   Mrs. Marshall writes:

He took with him £60[1] and a knapsack, and spent
most of the time walking in the high Alps.   This walking, summer after summer, turned him from a weak
into a strong man.   He left Cambridge early in June
jaded and overworked and returned in October brown
and strong and upright.   Carrying the knapsack pulled
him upright, and until he was over eighty he remained
so.   He even then exerted himself almost painfully to
hold himself straight.   When walking in the Alps his
practice was to get up at six and to be well on his way
before eight.   He would walk with knapsack on his
back for two or three hours.   He would then sit down,
sometimes on a glacier, and have a long pull at some
book—Goethe or Hegel or Kant or Herbert Spencer—
and then walk on to his next halting-place for the night.
This was in his philosophic stage.   Later on he worked
out his theories of Domestic and Foreign Trade in
these walks.   A large box of books, etc., was sent on
from one stage to another, but he would go for a week
or more just with a knapsack.   He would wash his shirt

[1] He used to reckon that his necessary expenditure as a bachelor
Fellow amounted to £300 a year, including £60 for vacation
travel.

SETTING OUT TO REVISE *THE PRINCIPLES*

Tyrol, 1901

by holding it in a fast-running stream and dry it by carrying it on his alpenstock over his shoulder. He did most of his hardest thinking in these solitary Alpine walks.

These *Wanderjahre* gave him a love for the Alps which he always retained, and even in 1920 (for the last time) we went to the South Tyrol, where he sat and worked in the high air.

Alfred always did his best work in the open air. When he became Fellow of St. John's he did his chief thinking between 10 A.M. and 2 P.M. and between 10 P.M. and 2 A.M. He had a monopoly of the Wilderness in the daytime and of the New Court Cloisters at night. At Palermo in the early eighties he worked on the roof of a quiet hotel, using the cover of the bath as an awning. At Oxford he made a "Den" in the garden in which he wrote. At Cambridge he worked in the balcony, and later in a large revolving shelter, fitted up as a study, called "The Ark", and in the Tyrol he arranged a heap of stones, a camp stool and an air cushion into what he called a "throne," and in later years we always carried a tent shelter with us, in which he spent the day.

In 1875 Marshall visited the United States for four months. He toured the whole of the East, and travelled as far as San Francisco. At Harvard and Yale he had long talks with the academic economists, and he had many introductions everywhere to leading citizens. But his chief purpose was the "study of the Problem of Protection in a New Country." About this he inquired on all hands, and towards the end of his trip was able to write in a letter home:

In Philadelphia I spent many hours in conversation with the leading protectionists. And now I think, as soon as I have read some books they have recommended me to read, I shall really know the whole of their case; and I do not believe there is or ever has been another Englishman who could say the same.

On his return to England he read a paper at the Cambridge Moral Science Club on American Industry, November 17, 1875, and later on he lectured at Bristol, in 1878, on "The Economic Condition of America." The American trip made on him a great impression, which coloured all his future work. He used to say that it was not so much what he actually learnt, as that he got to know what things he wanted to learn; that he was taught to see things in proportion; and that he was enabled to expect the coming supremacy of the United States, to know its causes and the directions it would take.

Meanwhile he had been helping Fawcett, who was professor, and Henry Sidgwick, to establish Political Economy as a serious study in the University of Cambridge. Two of his earliest pupils, H. S. Foxwell and, later on, my father, John Neville Keynes, who took the Moral Sciences Tripos in 1875, joined these three as lecturers on Political Economy in the University.

[*Photo. Frederick Hollyer*

MARY PALEY MARSHALL

1892

In 1876 Alfred Marshall became engaged to
Miss Mary Paley, a great-granddaughter of the
famous Archdeacon.   Miss Paley was a former
pupil of his and was a lecturer in Economics at
Newnham.[1]   His first book, *Economics of Industry*, published in 1879, was written in col-
laboration with her; indeed it had been, at the
start, her book and not his, having been undertaken by her at the request of a group of
Cambridge University Extensions lecturers.
They were married in 1877.   During forty-
seven years of married life his dependence upon
her devotion was complete.   Her life was given
to him and to his work with a degree of un-
selfishness and understanding that makes it
difficult for friends and old pupils to think of
them separately or to withhold from her shining
gifts of character a big share in what his intellect
accomplished.

Marriage, by involving the loss of his Fellowship, meant leaving Cambridge for a time,[2] and

[1] Miss Paley was one of the small band of five pioneers who,
before the foundation of Newnham College, came into residence
under Miss Clough in 1871 at 74 Regent Street, which had been
taken and furnished for the purpose by Henry Sidgwick.   She
and Miss Bulley, taking the Moral Sciences Tripos in 1874 as
Students of the "Association for Promoting the Higher Education
of Women in Cambridge," were the first of the group to take
honours at Cambridge.

[2] For a week or two Marshall entertained the idea of becoming
a candidate for the Esquire Bedellship at Cambridge, as a help

Marshall went to Bristol as the first Principal of University College, and as Professor of Political Economy.

Just at that time [Marshall has recorded] Balliol and New Colleges at Oxford were setting up at Bristol the first "University College": that is, a College designed to bring higher educational opportunities within the reach of the inhabitants of a large city, which had no University of its own. I was elected its first Principal: my wife lectured on Political Economy to a class consisting chiefly of ladies in the morning, and I lectured in the evening to a class composed chiefly of young business men.

Apart from his regular classes he gave a number of public evening lectures,[1] including a series on Henry George's *Progress and Poverty*. The work of the Marshalls at Bristol was much appreciated there, and the town kept up an interest in his career long after he had left it. But the administrative work, especially the business of begging money, which in view of the meagre endowments of the college was one of the main duties of the Principal, proved irksome and uncongenial. Soon after his marriage his health and nerves began to break

towards keeping himself. But "the more I look at the poker," he finally concluded, "the less I like it." He was actually, for a short time, Steward of St. John's.

[1] A lecture on "Water as an Element of National Wealth," which has been reprinted, is particularly interesting.

down, chiefly as a result of stone in the kidney. He was anxious to resign the position of Principal, but there was no convenient opportunity until 1881, when the appointment of Professor Ramsay to the Department of Chemistry provided a suitable successor. He went with his wife to Italy for nearly a year, working quietly on the roof of a small hotel at Palermo for five months and then moving to Florence and to Venice. He came back to Bristol, where he was still Professor of Political Economy, in 1882 with his health much restored; but he remained for the rest of his life somewhat hypochondriacal and inclined to consider himself on the verge of invalidism. In fact, his constitution was extremely tough and he remained in harness as a writer up to a very advanced age. But his nervous equilibrium was easily upset by unusual exertion or excitement or by controversy and difference of opinion; his power of continuous concentration on difficult mental work was inferior to his wishes, and he became dependent on a routine of life adapted even to his whims and fancies. In truth, he was haunted by a feeling that his physical strength and power of continuous concentration were inferior to the fields of work which he saw stretching ahead, and to the actual constructions he had conceived but not yet given to the world. By 1877, when he was thirty-five years of age, he had worked out within him the foundations of little less than a new science, of great consequence to mankind; and a collapse of health and strength during the five years following, when he should have been giving all this to the world, partly broke his courage, though not his determination.

Amongst the Governors of University College, Bristol, were Dr. Jowett, the Master of Balliol, and Professor Henry Smith, and these two were accustomed to stay with the Marshalls on their periodic visits to Bristol. Jowett's interest in Economics was always lively. While Tutor of Balliol he had given courses of set lectures on Political Economy, and he continued to direct individual undergraduates in the subject up to the end of his life.[1]   Jowett's interest and belief in Alfred Marshall were keenly

[1] In the charming little obituary of Jowett which Marshall contributed to the *Economic Journal* (vol. iii. p. 745), he wrote: "He took part in most of the questions which agitate modern economists; but his own masters were Plato and Ricardo. Everything that they said, and all that rose directly out of what they said, had a special interest for him. . . . In pure economics his favourite subject was the Currency, and he took a keen interest in the recent controversy on it.   His views were generally conservative; and he was never converted to bimetallism.   But he was ready to follow wherever Ricardo had pointed the way; and in a letter written not long ago he raised the question whether the world would not outgrow the use of gold as its standard of value, and adopt one of those artificial standards which vex the soul of Mr. Giffen."

aroused by the long evening talks which followed the meetings of the Governing Body,
and on the premature death of Arnold Toynbee
in 1883 he invited Marshall to take his place
as Fellow of Balliol and Lecturer in Political
Economy to the selected candidates for the
Indian Civil Service.[1]

Marshall's Oxford career was brief but
successful. He attracted able pupils, and his
public lectures were attended by larger and more
enthusiastic classes than at any other period
of his life. He encountered with credit, on
different occasions, Henry George and Hynd-
man in public debate, and was taking a prominent position in the University. In November
1884, however, Fawcett died, and in January
1885 Marshall returned to Cambridge as Professor of Political Economy.

IV

Marshall's serious study of Economic Theory
began in 1867; his characteristic doctrines were
far developed by 1875, and by 1883 they were
taking their final form. Nevertheless, no part
of his work was given to the world at large
in adequate shape until 1890 (*Principles of Eco-*

[1] Jowett always remained very fond of Alfred Marshall, and,
after the Marshalls left Oxford, it was with them that he generally
stayed on his visits to Cambridge.

nomics), and that part of the subject at which he had worked earliest and which was most complete by 1875, was not treated in a published book until nearly fifty years later, in 1923 (*Money, Credit and Commerce*). Meanwhile he had not kept his ideas to himself, but had shared them without reserve in lecture and in talk with friends and pupils. They leaked out to wider circles in privately printed pamphlets and through the writings of his pupils, and were extracted in cross-examination by Royal Commissions. Inevitably, when the books themselves appeared, they lacked the novelty and path-breaking powers which would have been acclaimed in them a generation earlier, and those economists all over the world who know Marshall only by his published work may find it difficult to understand the extraordinary position claimed for him by his English contemporaries and successors. It is proper, therefore, that I should make an attempt, necessarily imperfect from lack of full data, to trace the progress of his ideas, and then to set forth the reasons or the excuses for the unhappy delay in their publication.

Marshall's serious study of Economics began in 1867. To fix our ideas of date: Mill's *Political Economy* [1] had appeared in 1848; the

---

[1] What a contrast to Marshall's *Principles* the drafting of this

seventh edition, in 1871, was the last to receive
Mill's own corrections; and Mill died in 1873.
Das Kapital of Marx appeared in 1868; Jevons'
Theory of Political Economy [1] in 1871; Menger's
Grundsätze der Volkswirtschaftslehre also in
1871; Cairnes' *Leading Principles* in 1874.

Thus when Marshall began, Mill and
Ricardo still reigned supreme and unchallenged.
Roscher, of whom Marshall often spoke, was
the only other influence of importance. The
notion of applying mathematical methods was
in the air. But it had not yet yielded anything
substantial. Cournot's *Principes mathématiques
de la Théorie des Richesses* (1835) is mentioned
by Marshall in the Preface to the first edition of
the *Principles of Economics* as having particularly
influenced him; but I do not know at what date
this book first came into his hands.[2] This, and

famous book presents! Mill's *Political Economy* was commenced
in the autumn of 1845 and was ready for the press before the end
of 1847. In this period of little more than two years the work
was laid aside for six months while Mill was writing articles in
the *Morning Chronicle* (sometimes as many as five a week) on the
Irish Peasant problem. At the same time Mill was occupied all
day in the India Office. (See Mill's *Autobiography*.)

[1] Jevons' *Serious Fall in the Value of Gold ascertained, and its
Social Effects set forth*, had appeared in 1863 and his *Variation of
Prices* in 1865, from which two papers the modern method of
Index Numbers takes its rise. His main papers on the Periodicity
of Commercial Crises were later (1875–79).

[2] For a complete bibliography of early hints and foreshadow-
ings of mathematical treatment see the appendix to Irving Fisher's

the natural reaction of Ricardo on a Cambridge
mathematician of that date,[1] with perhaps some
hints of algebraical treatment in the arithmetical
examples of Mill's Book III. chap. xviii.[2] on
"International Values," were all that Marshall
had to go upon in the first instance. An
account of the progress of his thought from
1867 to his American trip in 1875, which
Marshall himself put into writing,[3] is appropriate at this point:

edition of Cournot's book. Fleeming Jenkin's brief paper of
1868 was not generally available until 1870, but was certainly
known to Marshall about that date (see his review of Jevons in
The Academy, 1872). Jevons' *Brief Account of a General Mathematical Theory of Political Economy* was presented to the Cambridge
Meeting of the British Association in 1862 and published in the
Statistical Journal in 1866; but this paper does not actually contain any mathematical treatment at all. Its purpose is to adum-
brate the idea of "the coefficient of utility" (*i.e.* final utility), and
to claim that this notion will allow the foundations of economics
to be worked out as a mathematical extension of the hedonistic
calculus.

[1] This was the age of Clerk Maxwell and W. K. Clifford, when
the children of the Mathematical Tripos were busy trying to
apply its apparatus to the experimental sciences. An extension to
the moral sciences was becoming obvious. Boole and Leslie Ellis,
a little earlier, were an important influence in the same direction.
Alfred Marshall, in 1867, trained as he was, an intimate of W. K.
Clifford, turning his attention to Ricardo, was *bound* to play
about with diagrams and algebra. No other explanations or
influences are needed.

[2] Particularly §§ 6-8, which were added by Mill to the third
edition (1852).

[3] This account was contributed by him to a German compilation of Portraits and Short Lives of leading Economists.

While still giving private lessons in mathematics,[1] he translated as many as possible of Ricardo's reasonings into mathematics; and he endeavoured to make them more general. Meanwhile he was attracted towards the new views of economics taken by Roscher and other German economists; and by Marx, Lassalle and other Socialists. But it seemed to him that the analytical methods of the historical economists were not always sufficiently thorough to justify their confidence that the causes which they assigned to economic events were the true causes. He thought indeed that the interpretation of the economic past was almost as difficult as the prediction of the future. The Socialists also seemed to him to underrate the difficulty of their problems, and to be too quick to assume that the abolition of private property would purge away the faults and deficiencies of human nature. . . . He set himself to get into closer contact with practical business and with the life of the working classes. On the one side he aimed at learning the broad features of the technique of every chief industry; and on the other he sought the society of trade unionists, co-operators and other working-class leaders. Seeing, however, that direct studies of life and work would not yield much fruit for many years, he decided to fill the interval by writing a separate monograph or special treatise on Foreign Trade; for the chief facts relating to it can be obtained from printed documents. He proposed that this should be the first of a group of monographs on special economic problems; and he hoped ultimately to compress these monographs into a general treatise of a similar scope to Mill's. After writing that larger treatise, but not before, he thought he might be ready to

[1] 1867.

write a short popular treatise. He has never changed his opinion that this is the best order of work; but his plans were overruled, and almost inverted, by the force of circumstances. He did indeed write the first draft of a monograph on Foreign Trade; and in 1875 he visited the chief seats of industry in America with the purpose of studying the problem of Protection in a new country. But this work was suspended by his marriage; and while engaged, in conjunction with his wife, in writing a short account of the Economics of Industry, forcibly simplified for working-class readers, he contracted an illness so serious that for some time he appeared unlikely to be able to do any more hard work. A little later he thought his strength might hold out for recasting his diagrammatic illustrations of economic problems. Though urged by the late Professor Walras about 1873 to publish these, he had declined to do so; because he feared that if separated from all concrete study of actual conditions, they might seem to claim a more direct bearing on real problems than they in fact had. He began, therefore, to supply some of the requisite limitations and conditions, and thus was written the kernel of the fifth book of his *Principles*. From that kernel the present volume was extended gradually backwards and forwards, till it reached the form in which it was published in 1890.

The fateful decision was the abandonment of the project to write "a group of monographs on special economic problems" in favour of a comprehensive treatise which should be born complete and fully armed from the head of an economic Jove—particularly when the special problems on which Marshall had worked first, Money and Foreign Trade, were held to occupy, logically, the latest sections of this treatise, with the result that they did not see the light for fifty years.

The evidence as to the order of his studies is as follows: In 1867 he began with the development of diagrammatic methods, with special regard to the problems of foreign trade, mainly under the influence of Ricardo and Mill. To this was added the influence of Cournot, and in a less degree that of von Thünen, by which he

was led to attach great importance to the fact that our observations of nature, in the moral as in the physical world, relate not so much to aggregate quantities, as to increments of quantities, and that in particular the demand for a thing is a continuous function, of which the "marginal" increment is, in stable equilibrium, balanced against the corresponding increment of its cost of production. It is not easy to get a clear full view of Continuity in this aspect without the aid either of mathematical symbols or of diagrams.[1]

By 1871 his progress along these lines was considerably advanced. He was expounding the new ideas to pupils and the foundations of his diagrammatic economics had been truly laid. In that year there appeared, as the result of independent work, Jevons' *Theory of Political*

[1] Preface to first edition of *Principles of Economics*.

Economy. The publication of this book must have been an occasion of some disappointment and annoyance to Marshall. It took the cream of novelty off the new ideas which Marshall was slowly working up without giving them—in Marshall's judgement—adequate or accurate treatment. Nevertheless, it undoubtedly gave Jevons priority of publication as regards the group of ideas connected with "marginal" (or, as Jevons called it, "final") utility. Marshall's references to the question of priority are extremely reserved. He is careful to leave Jevons' claim undisputed, whilst pointing out, indirectly, but quite clearly and definitely, that his own work owed little or nothing to Jevons.[1]

---

[1] See, particularly, (1) his footnote relating to his use of the term "marginal" (Preface to *Principles*, 1st ed.), where he implies that the word was suggested to him, as a result of reading von Thünen (though von Thünen does not actually use the word), *before* Jevons' book appeared (in his British Association paper of 1862, published in 1866, Jevons uses the term "coefficient of utility"), that, after its appearance, he temporarily deferred to Jevons and adopted his word "final" (*e.g.* in the first *Economics of Industry*), and that later on he reverted to his original phrase as being the better (it is also an almost literal equivalent of Menger's word "Grenznutzen"); and (2) his footnote to bk. iii. chap. vi. § 3 on Consumers' Rent (or Surplus), where he writes (my italics): "The notion of an exact measurement of Consumers' Rent was published by Dupuit in 1844. But his work was forgotten; and the first to publish a clear analysis of the relation of total to marginal (or final) utility in the English language was Jevons in 1871, when he had not read Dupuit. The notion of Consumers' Rent was suggested *to the present writer* by a study of the mathe-

In 1872 Marshall reviewed [1] Jevons' *Political Economy* in *The Academy*.   This review,[2] while not unfavourable, is somewhat cool and it points out several definite errors:

The main value of the book [it concludes] does not lie in its more prominent theories, but in its original treatment of a number of minor points, its suggestive remarks and careful analyses. We continually meet with old friends in new dresses. . . . Thus it is a familiar truth that the total utility of any commodity is not proportional to its final degree of utility. . . . But Prof. Jevons has made this the leading idea of the costume in which he has displayed a large number of economic facts.

When, however, Marshall came, in later years, to write the *Principles*, his desire to be scrupulously fair to Jevons and to avoid the least sign of jealousy is very marked.   It is true that in one passage [3] he writes: "It is unfortunate that here as elsewhere Jevons' delight in stating his case strongly has led him to a conclusion, which not only is inaccurate, but does mischief. . . ."

matical aspects of demand and utility under the influence of Cournot, von Thünen, and Bentham."

[1] I believe that Marshall only wrote two reviews in the whole of his life—this review of Jevons in 1872, and a review of Edgeworth's *Mathematical Psychics* in 1881.

[2] The main interest of the review, which is, so far as I am aware, A. M.'s first appearance in print (at thirty years of age), is, perhaps, the many respects in which it foreshadows his permanent attitude to his subject.   [3] P. 166 (3rd ed.).

But he says elsewhere:[1] "There are few writers
of modern times who have approached as near
to the brilliant originality of Ricardo as Jevons
has done," and "There are few thinkers whose
claims on our gratitude are as high and as
various as those of Jevons."

In truth, Jevons' *Theory of Political Economy*
is a brilliant but hasty, inaccurate, and incomplete brochure, as far removed as possible from
the painstaking, complete, ultra-conscientious,
ultra-unsensational methods of Marshall.   It
brings out unforgettably the notions of final
utility and of the balance between the disutility
of labour and the utility of the product.   But it
lives merely in the tenuous world of bright
ideas[2] when we compare it with the great working machine evolved by the patient, persistent
toil and scientific genius of Marshall.   Jevons
saw the kettle boil and cried out with the
delighted voice of a child; Marshall too had
seen the kettle boil and sat down silently to
build an engine.

Meanwhile, Marshall worked on at the generalised diagrammatic scheme disclosed in his
papers on the Pure Theory of Foreign Trade

[1] In the *Note on Ricardo's Theory of Value*, which is, in the
main, a reply to Jevons.

[2] How disappointing are the fruits, now that we have them, of
the bright idea of reducing Economics to a mathematical application of the hedonistic calculus of Bentham!

and Domestic Values. These must have been substantially complete about 1873 and were communicated to his pupils (particularly to Sir H. H. Cunynghame) about that date. They were drafted as non-consecutive [1] chapters of *The Theory of Foreign Trade, with some Allied Problems relating to the Doctrine of Laisser Faire*, which he nearly completed in 1875–77 after his return from America, embodying the results of his work from 1869 onwards.[2] In 1877 he turned aside to write the *Economics of Industry* with Mrs. Marshall. In 1879 Henry Sidgwick, alarmed at the prospect of Marshall's right of priority being taken from him, printed them for private circulation and copies were sent to leading economists at home and abroad.[3] These chapters, which are now very scarce in their original form, were never published to the world at large,[4] but the most significant parts of them were incorporated in Book V. chaps.

---

[1] The last proposition of *Foreign Trade* (which comes first) is Prop. XIII.; the first of *Domestic Values* is Prop. XVII.

[2] "Chiefly between 1869 and 1873"—see *Money, Credit and Commerce*, p. 330.

[3] See the Preface to the first edition of the *Principles*. Jevons refers to them in the second edition of his *Theory*, published in 1879; and Pantaleoni reproduced much of them in his *Principii di Economia Pura* (1889).

[4] The London School of Economics published a facsimile reprint of these two papers in 1930 as No. 1 in their series of *Reprints of Scarce Tracts in Economic and Political Science*.

xi. and xii. of the *Principles of Economics*, and (fifty years after their origination) in Appendix J of *Money, Credit and Commerce*.

Marshall's mathematical and diagrammatic exercises in Economic Theory were of such a character in their grasp, comprehensiveness, and scientific accuracy, and went so far beyond the "bright ideas" of his predecessors, that we may justly claim him as the founder of modern diagrammatic economics—that elegant apparatus which generally exercises a powerful attraction on clever beginners, which all of us use as an inspirer of, and a check on, our intuitions and as a shorthand record of our results, but which generally falls into the background as we penetrate further into the recesses of the subject. The fact that Marshall's results percolated to the outer world a drop at a time, and reached in their complete form only a limited circle, lost him much international fame which would otherwise have been his, and even, perhaps, retarded the progress of the subject. Nevertheless, we can, I think, on reflection understand Marshall's reluctance to open his career with publishing his diagrammatic apparatus by itself.

For, whilst it was a necessary appurtenance of his intellectual approach to the subject, an appearance of emphasising or exalting such methods pointed right away from what he regarded, quite early in his life, as the proper attitude to economic inquiry. Moreover, Marshall, as one who had been Second Wrangler and had nourished ambitions to explore molecular physics, always felt a slight contempt from the intellectual or aesthetic point of view for the rather "potty" scraps of elementary algebra, geometry, and differential calculus which make up mathematical economics.[1] Unlike physics, for example, such parts of the bare bones of economic theory as are expressible in mathematical form are extremely easy compared with the economic interpretation of the complex and incompletely known facts of experience,[2] and

[1] Mathematical economics often exercise an excessive fascination and influence over students who approach the subject without much previous training in technical mathematics. They are so easy as to be within the grasp of almost anyone, yet do introduce the student, on a small scale, to the delights of perceiving constructions of pure form, and place toy bricks in his hands that he can manipulate for himself, which gives a new thrill to those who have had no glimpse of the sky-scraping architecture and minutely embellished monuments of modern mathematics.

[2] Professor Planck, of Berlin, the famous originator of the Quantum Theory, once remarked to me that in early life he had thought of studying economics, but had found it too difficult! Professor Planck could easily master the whole corpus of mathematical economics in a few days. He did not mean that! But the amalgam of logic and intuition and the wide knowledge of facts, most of which are not precise, which is required for economic interpretation in its highest form is, quite truly, overwhelmingly difficult for those whose gift mainly consists in the power to

lead one but a very little way towards establishing useful results.

Marshall felt all this with a vehemence which not all his pupils have shared. The preliminary mathematics was for him child's play. He wanted to enter the vast laboratory of the world, to hear its roar and distinguish the several notes, to speak with the tongues of business men, and yet to observe all with the eyes of a highly intelligent angel. So "he set himself," as is recorded in his own words above (p. 329), "to get into closer contact with practical business and with the life of the working classes."

 Thus Marshall, having begun by founding modern diagrammatic methods, ended by using much self-obliteration to keep them in their proper place. When the *Principles* appeared, the diagrams were imprisoned in footnotes, or, at their freest, could but exercise themselves as in a yard within the confines of a brief Appendix. As early as 1872, in reviewing Jevons' *Political Economy*, he wrote:

We owe several valuable suggestions to the many investigations in which skilled mathematicians, English and continental, have applied their favourite method to the treatment of economical problems. But all that has been important in their reasonings and results has, with

imagine and pursue to their furthest points the implications and prior conditions of comparatively simple facts which are known with a high degree of precision.

scarcely an exception, been capable of being described in ordinary language. . . . The book before us would be improved if the mathematics were omitted, but the diagrams retained.

In 1881, reviewing Edgeworth's *Mathematical Psychics*, after beginning "This book shows clear signs of genius, and is a promise of great things to come," he adds, "It will be interesting, in particular, to see how far he succeeds in preventing his mathematics from running away with him, and carrying him out of sight of the actual facts of economics." And finally, in 1890, in the Preface to the *Principles*, he first emphasises his preference for diagrams over algebra, then allows the former a limited usefulness[1] and reduces the latter to the position of a convenience for private use.[2]

In his reaction against excessive addiction to these methods, and also (a less satisfactory motive) from fear of frightening "business men"

[1] "The argument in the text is never dependent on them; and they may be omitted; but experience seems to show that they give a firmer grasp of many important principles than can be got without their aid; and that there are many problems of pure theory, which no one who has once learnt to use diagrams will willingly handle in any other way."

[2] "The chief use of pure mathematics in economic questions seems to be in helping a person to write down quickly, shortly and exactly, some of his thoughts for his own use. . . . It seems doubtful whether anyone spends his time well in reading lengthy translations of economic doctrines into mathematics, that have not been made by himself."

away from reading his book, Marshall may have gone too far. After all, if "there are many problems of pure theory, which no one who has once learnt to use diagrams will willingly handle in any other way," such diagrams must surely form a part of every advanced course in economics,[1] and they should be available for students in the fullest and clearest form possible.[2]

Whilst, however, Marshall's reluctance to print the results of his earliest investigations is mainly explained by the profundity of his insight into the true character of his subject in its highest and most useful developments, and by his unwillingness to fall short of his own ideals in what he gave to the world, it was a great pity that *The Theory of Foreign Trade, with some Allied Problems relating to the Doctrine of Laisser Faire*, did not see the light in 1877, even in an imperfect form.[3] After all, he had originally

[1] Marshall himself always used them freely in his lectures.

[2] Two former pupils of Marshall's, Sir Henry Cunynghame and Mr. A. W. Flux, have done something to supply the want. But we still, after fifty years, lack the ideal text-book for this purpose. Professor Bowley's lately published *Mathematical Groundwork of Economics* runs somewhat counter to Marshall's precepts by preferring, on the whole, algebraical to diagrammatic methods.

[3] Indeed, it is not very clear why he abandoned the publication of this book. Certainly up to the middle of 1877 he still intended to publish it. My father noted in his diary on February 8, 1877: "Marshall has brought me part of the MS. of a book on foreign

embarked on this particular inquiry because, in this case, "the chief facts relating to it can be obtained from printed documents"; and these facts, supplemented by those which he had obtained first-hand during his visit to the United States about the actual operation of Protection in a new country, might have been deemed sufficient for a monograph. The explanation is partly to be found in the fact that, when his health broke down, he believed that he had only a few years to live and that these must be given to the working out of his fundamental ideas on Value and Distribution.

We must regret still more Marshall's postponement of the publication of his *Theory of Money* until extreme old age, when time had deprived his ideas of freshness and his exposition of sting and strength. There is no part of Economics where Marshall's originality and priority of thought are more marked than here,

trade that he is writing, for me to look over." Both Sidgwick and Jevons had also read it in manuscript, and had formed a high opinion of it, as appears from their testimonials written in June 1877, when Marshall was applying for the Bristol appointment. Sidgwick wrote: "I doubt not that his forthcoming work, of which the greater part is already completed, will give him at once a high position among living English economists." And Jevons: "Your forthcoming work on the theory of Foreign Trade is looked forward to with much interest by those acquainted with its contents, and will place you among the most original writers on the science."

or where his superiority of insight and knowledge over his contemporaries was greater.

Here too was a semi-independent section
of the subject ideally suited to separate treatment in a monograph. Yet apart from what
is embedded in his evidence before Royal Commissions and occasional articles, not one single
scrap was given to the world in his own
words and his own atmosphere at the right
time. Since *Money* was from the early seventies onwards one of his favourite topics for
lectures, his main ideas became known to pupils
in a general way,[1] with the result that there grew
up at Cambridge an oral tradition, first from
Marshall's own lectures and after his retirement
from those of Professor Pigou, different from,
and (I think it may be claimed) superior to, anything that could be found in printed books until
recently.[2] It may be convenient at this point
to attempt a brief summary of Marshall's main
contributions to Monetary Theory.

Marshall printed nothing whatever on the
subject of Money [3] previously to the Bimetallic

[1] His unsystematic method of lecturing prevented the average,
and even the superior, student from getting down in his notes
anything very consecutive or complete.

[2] Professor Irving Fisher has been the first, in several instances,
to publish in book-form ideas analogous to those which had been
worked out by Marshall at much earlier dates.

[3] The *Economics of Industry* (1879) was not intended to cover
this part of the subject and contains only a brief reference to

controversy, and even then he waited a considerable time before he intervened. His first serious contribution to the subject was contained in his answers to a questionnaire printed by the Royal Commission on the Depression of Trade and Industry in 1886. This was followed by his article on "Remedies for Fluctuations of General Prices" in the *Contemporary Review* for March 1887, and a little later by his voluminous evidence before the Gold and Silver Commission in 1887 and 1888. In 1899 came his evidence before the Indian Currency Committee. But his theories were not expounded in a systematic form until the appearance of *Money, Credit and Commerce* in 1923. By this date nearly all his main ideas had found expression in the works of others. He had passed his eightieth year; his strength was no longer equal to much more than piecing together earlier fragments; and its jejune treatment, carefully avoiding difficulties and complications, yields the mere shadow of what he had had it in him to bring forth twenty [1] or (better) thirty years earlier. It happens, however, that the earliest extant manuscript of Marshall's, written about 1871, deals

it. The references to the Trade Cycle in this book are, however, important.

[1] I can speak on this matter from personal recollection, since is was only a little later than this (in 1906) that I attended his lectures on Money.

with his treatment of the Quantity Theory. It is a remarkable example of the continuity of his thought from its first beginnings between 1867 and 1877, that the whole of the substance of Book I. chap. iv. of his *Money, Credit and Commerce* is to be found here, worked out with fair completeness and with much greater strength of exposition and illustration than he could manage fifty years later. I have no evidence at what date he had arrived at the leading ideas underlying his *Contemporary Review* article or his evidence before the Gold and Silver Commission.[1] But the passages about Commercial Crises in the *Economics of Industry*, from which he quoted freely in his reply to the Trade Depression Commissioners, show that he was on the same lines of thought in 1879. The following are the most important and characteristic of Marshall's original contributions to this part of Economics.

(1) *The exposition of the Quantity Theory of Money as a part of the General Theory of Value.* He always taught that the value of money is a function of its supply on the one hand, and the demand for it, on the other, as measured by "the average stock of command over commodities which each person cares to keep in a ready

[1] In expounding his "Symmetallism" to the Commissioners he said (Q. 9837): "I have a bimetallic hobby of my own. . . . I have had it by me now for more than 10 years"—which brings this particular train of thought back to before 1878.

form." He went on to explain how each individual decides how much to keep in a ready form as the result of a *balance* of advantage between this and alternative forms of wealth.

The exchange value of the whole amount of coin in the Kingdom [he wrote in the manuscript of 1871 mentioned above] is just equal to that of the whole amount of the commodities over which the members of the community have decided to keep a command in this ready form. Thus with a silver currency if we know the number of ounces of silver in circulation we can determine what the value of one ounce of silver will be in terms of other commodities by dividing the value of above given amount of commodities by the number of ounces. Suppose that on the average each individual in a community chose to keep command over commodities in a ready form to the extent of one-tenth of his year's income. The money, supposed in this case exclusively silver, in the Kingdom will be equal in value to one-tenth of the annual income of the kingdom. Let their habits alter, each person being willing, for the sake of gain in other ways, to be to a greater extent without the power of having each want satisfied as soon as it arises. Let on the average each person choose to keep command over commodities in a ready form only to the extent of a twentieth part of his income. So much silver as before not being wanted at the old value, it will fall in value. It would accordingly be more used in manufactures, while its production from the mines would be checked. . . .[1]

[1] When I attended his lectures in 1906 he used to illustrate this theory with some very elegant diagrams.

He points out that the great advantage of this
method of approach is that it avoids the awkward conception of "rapidity of circulation"
(though he is able to show the exact logical
relation between the two conceptions): "When,
however, we try to establish a connection between 'the rapidity of circulation' and the value
of money, it introduces grave complications.
Mr. Mill is aware of the evil (*Political Economy*,
Book III. chap. viii. § 3, latter part), but he has
not pointed the remedy." [1] Marshall also
expounded long ago the way in which distrust
of a currency raises prices by diminishing the
willingness of the public to hold stocks of it—a
phenomenon to which recent events have now
called everyone's attention; and he was aware
that the fluctuation in the price level, which
is an accompaniment of the trade cycle,
corresponds to a fluctuation in the volume
of "ready command" [2] which the public desire
to hold.

(2) *The distinction between the "real" rate of
interest and the "money" rate of interest, and the
relevance of this to the credit cycle, when the value
of money is fluctuating.* The first clear exposition of this is, I think, that given in the *Prin-*

[1] This extract, as well as that given above, is from the manuscript of 1871.

[2] This is Marshall's phrase for what I have called "real
balances."

ciples (1890), Book VI. chap. vi. (concluding note).[1]

(3) *The causal train by which, in modern credit systems, an additional supply of money influences prices, and the part played by the rate of discount.* The *locus classicus* for an account of this, and the only detailed account for many years to which students could be referred, is Marshall's Evidence before the Gold and Silver Commission, 1887 (particularly the earlier part of his evidence), supplemented by his Evidence before the Indian Currency Committee, 1899. It was an odd state of affairs that one of the most fundamental parts of Monetary Theory should, for about a quarter of century, have been available to students nowhere except embedded in the form of question-and-answer before a Government Commission interested in a transitory practical problem.

(4) *The enunciation of the "Purchasing Power Parity" Theory as determining the rate of exchange between countries with mutually inconvertible currencies.* In substance this theory is due to Ricardo, but Professor Cassel's restatement of it in a form applicable to modern conditions was

---

[1] In repeating the substance of this Note to the Indian Currency Committee (1899) he refers in generous terms to the then recent elaboration of the idea in Professor Irving Fisher's *Appreciation and Interest* (1896). See also for some analogous ideas Marshall's first *Economics of Industry* (1879), bk. iii. chap. i. §§ 5, 6.

anticipated by Marshall in the memorandum [1]
appended to his Evidence before the Gold and
Silver Commission (1888). It also had an important place in the conclusions which he laid
before the Indian Currency Committee in 1899.
The following from an abstract of his opinions
handed in by Marshall to the Gold and Silver
Commission gives his theory in a nutshell: "Let
B have an inconvertible paper-currency (say
roubles). In each country prices will be
governed by the relation between the volume of
the currency and the work it has to do. The
gold price of the rouble will be fixed by the
course of trade just at the ratio which gold prices
in A bear to rouble prices in B (allowing for cost
of carriage)."

(5) *The "chain" method of compiling index-
numbers.* The first mention of this method is in
a footnote to the last section (entitled *How to
Estimate a Unit of Purchasing Power*) of his

---

[1] Entitled *Memorandum as to the Effects which Differences
between the Currencies of different Nations have on International
Trade.* His illustrations are in terms of English gold and Russian
paper roubles; and alternatively of English gold and Indian
silver. He argues that a prolonged departure from purchasing
power parity (he does not use this term) is not likely except when
there is "a general distrust of Russia's economic future, which
makes investors desire to withdraw their capital from Russia"—
a remarkable prevision of recent events. A portion of this
Memorandum was reproduced as the first part of Appendix G of
Money, Credit and Commerce.

"Remedies for Fluctuations of General Prices"
(1887).

(6) *The proposal of paper currency for the
circulation (on the lines of Ricardo's "Proposals for
an Economical and Secure Currency") based on
gold-and-silver symmetallism as the standard.* This
suggestion is first found in his reply to the Commissioners on Trade Depression in 1886. He
argued that ordinary bimetallism would always
tend to work out as alternative-metallism.

I submit [he went on] that, if we are to have a great
disturbance of our currency for the sake of bi-metallism,
we ought to be sure that we get it. . . . My alternative
scheme is got from his (Ricardo's) simply by wedding a
bar of silver of, say, 2000 grammes to a bar of gold of,
say, 100 grammes; the government undertaking to be
always ready to buy or sell a wedded pair of bars for a
fixed amount of currency. . . . This plan could be
started by any nation without waiting for the concur-
rence of others.

He did not urge the immediate adoption of
this system, but put it forward as being at least
preferable to bimetallism. The same proposal was repeated in 1887 in his article on
"Remedies for Fluctuations of General Prices,"
and in 1888 in his Evidence before the Gold and
Silver Commission.[1]

(7) *The proposal of an official Tabular Standard*

---

[1] See also *Money, Credit and Commerce*, pp. 64-67.

for optional use in the case of long contracts. This proposal first appears in an appendix to a paper on remedies for the discontinuity of employment, which Marshall read at the "Industrial Remuneration Conference" in 1885.[1] He repeated, and added to, what he had said there, in his Reply to the Commissioners on Trade Depression in 1886.

A great cause of the discontinuity of industry [he wrote] is the want of certain knowledge as to what a pound is going to be worth a short time hence. . . . This serious evil can be much diminished by a plan which economists have long advocated. In proposing this remedy I want government to help business, though not to do business. It should publish tables showing as closely as may be the changes in the purchasing power of gold, and should facilitate contracts for payments to be made in terms of units of fixed purchasing power. . . . The unit of constant general purchasing power would be applicable, at the free choice of both parties concerned, for nearly all contracts for the payment of interest, and for the repayment of loans; and for many contracts for rent, and for wages and salaries. . . . I wish to emphasise the fact that this proposal is independent of the form of our currency, and does not ask for any change in it. I admit that the plan would seldom be available for the purposes of international trade. But its importance as a steadying influence to our home trade

[1] Entitled "How far do remediable causes influence prejudicially (*a*) the continuity of employment, (*b*) the rates of wages?"

could be so great, and its introduction would be so easy and so free from the evils which generally surround the interference of Government in business, that I venture to urge strongly its claims on your immediate attention.

This important proposal was further developed in Marshall's remarkable essay on "Remedies for Fluctuations of General Prices," which has been mentioned above. The first three sections of this essay are entitled: I. *The Evils of a Fluctuating Standard of Value*; II. *The Precious Metals cannot afford a good Standard of Value*; III. *A Standard of Value independent of Gold and Silver*. Marshall had a characteristic habit in all his writings of reserving for footnotes what was most novel or important in what he had to say,[1] and the following is an extract from a footnote to this essay:

Every plan for regulating the supply of the currency, so that its value shall be constant, must, I think, be national and not international. I will indicate briefly two such plans, though I do not advocate either of them. On the first plan the currency would be inconvertible. An automatic Government Department would buy Consols for currency whenever £1 was worth more than a unit, and would sell Consols for currency whenever it was worth less. . . . The other plan is that of a convertible currency, each £1 note giving the right to demand at a

---

[1] It would almost be better to read the footnotes and appendices of Marshall's big volumes and omit the text, rather than *vice versa*.

Government Office as much gold as at that time had the value of half a unit together with as much silver as had the value of half a unit.[1]

The *Economist* mocked at Symmetallism and the optional Tabular Standard; and Marshall, always a little over-afraid of being thought unpractical or above the head of the "business man" (that legendary monster), did not persevere.[2]

V

I promised, above, that I would endeavour to set forth the reasons or the excuses for the delay in the publication of Marshall's methods and theories concerning Diagrammatic Methods, the Theory of Foreign Trade, and the Principles

[1] The last part of this sentence presumes the adoption of Symmetallism. The second plan is akin to Prof. Irving Fisher's "Compensated Dollar."

[2] In December 1923, after I had sent him my *Tract on Monetary Reform*, he wrote to me: "As years go on it seems to become ever clearer that there ought to be an international currency; and that the—in itself foolish—superstition that gold is the 'natural' representative of value has done excellent service. I have appointed myself amateur currency-mediciner; but I cannot give myself even a tolerably good testimonial in that capacity. And I am soon to go away; but, if I have opportunity, I shall ask newcomers to the celestial regions whether you have succeeded in finding a remedy for currency-maladies." As regards the choice between the advantages of a national and of an international currency I think that what he wrote in 1887 was the truer word, and that a constant-value currency must be, in the first instance at least, a national currency.

of Money and Credit. I think that the reasons, some of which apply to all periods of his life, were partly good and partly bad. Let us take the good ones first.

Marshall, as already pointed out above, arrived very early at the point of view that the bare bones of economic theory are not worth much in themselves and do not carry one far in the direction of useful, practical conclusions. The whole point lies in applying them to the interpretation of current economic life. This requires a profound knowledge of the actual facts of industry and trade. But these, and the relation of individual men to them, are constantly and rapidly changing. Some extracts from his Inaugural Lecture at Cambridge [1] will indicate his position:

The change that has been made in the point of view of Economics by the present generation is due to the discovery that man himself is in a great measure a creature of circumstances and changes with them. The chief fault in English economists at the beginning of the century was not that they ignored history and statistics, but that they regarded man as so to speak a constant quantity, and gave themselves little trouble to study his variations. They therefore attributed to the forces of supply and demand a much more mechanical and regular action than they actually have. Their most vital fault was that they did not see how liable to change are the

[1] *The Present Position of Economics*, 1885.

habits and institutions of industry. But the Socialists were men who had felt intensely, and who knew something about the hidden springs of human action of which the economists took no account. Buried among their wild rhapsodies there were shrewd observations and pregnant suggestions from which philosophers and economists had much to learn. Among the bad results of the narrowness of the work of English economists early in the century, perhaps the most unfortunate was the opportunity which it gave to sciolists to quote and misapply economic dogmas. Ricardo and his chief followers did not make clear to others, it was not even quite clear to themselves, that what they were building up was not universal truth, but machinery of universal application in the discovery of a certain class of truths. While attributing high and transcendent universality to the central scheme of economic reasoning, I do not assign any universality to economic dogmas. It is not a body of concrete truth, but an engine for the discovery of concrete truth.[1]

Holding these views and living at a time of reaction against economists when the faults of his predecessors, to which he draws attention above, were doing their maximum amount of harm, he was naturally reluctant to publish the isolated apparatus of economics, divorced from its appropriate applications. Diagrams and pure theory by themselves might do more harm

---

[1] This is a portmanteau quotation—I have run together non-consecutive passages. Parts of this lecture were transcribed almost verbatim in the *Principles*, bk. i. chap. iv.

than good, by increasing the confusion between the objects and methods of the mathematical sciences and those of the social sciences, and would give what he regarded as just the wrong emphasis. In publishing his intellectual exercises without facing the grind of discovering their points of contact with the real world he would be following and giving bad example. On the other hand, the relevant facts were extremely hard to come by—much harder than now. The progress of events in the seventies and eighties, particularly in America, was extraordinarily rapid, and organised sources of information, of which there are now so many, scarcely existed. In the twenty years from 1875 to 1895 he was, in fact, greatly increasing his command over real facts and his power of economic judgement, and the work which he could have published between 1875 and 1885 would have been much inferior to what he was capable of between 1885 and 1895.

The other valid reason was a personal one. At the critical moment of his life his health was impaired. After health was restored, the preparation of lectures and the time he devoted to his pupils made big interruptions in the writing of books. He was too meticulous in his search for accuracy, and also for conciseness of expression, to be a ready writer. He was particularly

P

unready in the business of fitting pieces into a big whole and of continually rewriting them in the light of their reactions on and from the other pieces. He was always trying to write big books, yet lacked the power of rapid execution and continuous concentration (such as J. S. Mill had) and that of continuous artistic sensibility to the whole (such as Adam Smith had) which are necessary for the complete success of a Treatise.

We are now approaching in our explanations what we must admit as bad reasons.   Given his views as to the impossibility of any sort of finality in Economics and as to the rapidity with which events change, given the limitations of his own literary aptitudes and of his leisure for book-making, was it not a fatal decision to abandon his first intention of separate independent monographs in favour of a great Treatise?   I think that it was, and that certain weaknesses contributed to it.

Marshall was conscious of the great superiority of his powers over those of his surviving contemporaries.   In his Inaugural lecture of 1885 he said: "Twelve years ago England possessed perhaps the ablest set of economists that there have ever been in a country at one time.   But one after another there have been taken from us Mill, Cairnes, Bagehot, Cliffe

Leslie, Jevons, Newmarch, and Fawcett."
There was no one left who could claim at that
date to approach Marshall in stature. To his
own pupils, who were to carry on the Economics
of the future, Marshall was ready to devote time
and strength. But he was too little willing to
cast his half-baked bread on the waters, to trust
in the efficacy of the co-operation of many
minds, and to let the big world draw from him
what sustenance it could. Was he not attempting, contrary to his own principles, to achieve
an impossible finality? An Economic Treatise
may have great educational value. Perhaps we
require one treatise, as a *pièce de résistance*, for
each generation. But in view of the transitory
character of economic facts, and the bareness of
economic principles in isolation, does not the
progress and the daily usefulness of economic
science require that pioneers and innovators
should eschew the Treatise and prefer the
pamphlet or the monograph? I depreciated
Jevons' *Political Economy* above on the ground
that it was no more than a brilliant brochure.
Yet it was Jevons' willingness to spill his ideas,
to flick them at the world, that won him his great
personal position and his unrivalled power of
stimulating other minds. Every one of Jevons'
contributions to Economics was in the nature
of a pamphlet. Malthus spoilt the *Essay on*

Population when, after the first edition, he converted it into a Treatise. Ricardo's greatest works were written as ephemeral pamphlets. Did not Mill, in achieving by his peculiar gifts a successful Treatise, do more for pedagogics than for science, and end by sitting like an Old Man of the Sea on the voyaging Sinbads of the next generation? [1] Economists must leave to Adam Smith alone the glory of the Quarto, must pluck the day, fling pamphlets into the wind, write always *sub specie temporis*, and achieve immortality by accident, if at all.

Moreover, did not Marshall, by keeping his wisdom at home until he could produce it fully clothed, mistake, perhaps, the true nature of his own special gift? "Economics," he said, in the passage quoted above, "is not a body of concrete truth, but an engine for the discovery of concrete truth." This engine, as we employ it to-day, is largely Marshall's creation. He put it in the hands of his pupils long before he offered it to the world. The building of this engine was the essential achievement of Marshall's peculiar genius. Yet he hankered greatly after the "concrete truth" which he had disclaimed and for the discovery of which he was not specially qualified. I have very early memories, almost

---

[1] How Jevons hated Mill, just because he had been compelled to lecture on Mill's *Political Economy* as a Gospel Text-book!

before I knew what Economics meant, of the sad complaints of my father, who had been able to observe as pupil and as colleague the progress of Marshall's thought almost from the beginning, of Marshall's obstinate refusal to understand where his special strength and weakness really lay, and of how his unrealisable ambitions stood in the way of his giving to the world the true treasures of his mind and genius. Economics all over the world might have progressed much faster, and Marshall's authority and influence would have been far greater, if his temperament had been a little different.

Two other characteristics must be mentioned. First, Marshall was too much afraid of being wrong, too thin-skinned towards criticism, too easily upset by controversy even on matters of minor importance. An extreme sensitiveness deprived him of magnanimity towards the critic or the adversary. This fear of being open to correction by speaking too soon aggravated other tendencies. Yet, after all, there is no harm in being sometimes wrong—especially if one is promptly found out. Nevertheless, this quality was but the defect of the high standard he never relaxed—which touched his pupils with awe—of scientific accuracy and truth.

Second, Marshall was too anxious to do good. He had an inclination to undervalue those intellectual parts of the subject which were not *directly* connected with human well-being or the condition of the working classes or the like, although *indirectly* they might be of the utmost importance, and to feel that when he was pursuing them he was not occupying himself with the Highest.   It came out of the conflict, already remarked, between an intellect, which was hard, dry, critical, as unsentimental as you could find, with emotions and, generally unspoken, aspirations of quite a different type. When his intellect chased diagrams and Foreign Trade and Money there was an evangelical moraliser of an imp somewhere inside him that was so ill-advised as to disapprove.   Near the end of his life, when the intellect grew dimmer and the preaching imp could rise nearer to the surface to protest against its lifelong servitude, he once said: "If I had to live my life over again I should have devoted it to psychology.   Economics has too little to do with ideals.   If I said much about them I should not be read by business men."   But these notions had always been with him.   He used to tell the following story of his early life: "About the time that I first resolved to make as thorough a study as I could of Political Economy (the word Economics was not then invented) I saw in a shopwindow a small oil painting [of a man's face

with a strikingly gaunt and wistful expression,
as of one 'down and out'] and bought it for a
few shillings. I set it up above the chimney-
piece in my room in college and thenceforward
called it my patron saint, and devoted myself
to trying how to fit men like that for heaven.
Meanwhile, I got a good deal interested in the
semi-mathematical side of pure Economics, and
was afraid of becoming a mere thinker. But a
glance at my patron saint seemed to call me
back to the right path. That was particularly
useful after I had been diverted from the study
of ultimate aims to the questions about Bimetallism, etc., which at one time were dominant. I
despised them, but the 'instinct of the chase'
tempted me towards them." This was the
defect of that other great quality of his which
always touched his pupils—his immense disinterestedness and public spirit.

VI

At any rate, in 1877 Marshall turned aside
to help his wife with the *Economics of Industry*
(published in 1879), designed as a manual
for Cambridge University Extension lecturers,
which, as it progressed, became more and more
his work. In later years Marshall grew very
unfriendly to the little book. After the publication of the *Principles* he suppressed it and

replaced it in 1892 with an almost wholly different book under the same title, which was mainly an abridgement of the *Principles* and "an attempt to adapt it to the needs of junior students." Marshall's feelings were due, I think, to the fact that his theory of value, which was here first published to the world, was necessarily treated in a brief and imperfect manner, yet remained for eleven years all that the outside world had to judge from. His controversies in the *Quarterly Journal of Economics* in 1887 and 1888 with American economists who had read the little book accentuated this feeling. He also revolted later on from the conception of Economics as a subject capable of being treated in a light and simple manner for elementary students by half-instructed Extension lecturers [1] aided by half-serious books. "This volume," he wrote in 1910 to a Japanese translator of the 1879 book, "was begun in the hope that it might be possible to combine simplicity with scientific accuracy. But though a simple book can be written on selected topics, the central doctrines of Economics are not simple and cannot be made so."

[1] So far, however, from being out of sympathy with the ideals underlying the Extension Movement (or its modern variant the W.E.A.), Marshall had been connected with it from the beginning, and had himself given Extension Courses at Bristol for five years.

Yet these sentiments do a real injustice to the book. It won high praise from competent judges and was, during the whole of its life, much the best little text-book available.[1] If we are to have an elementary text-book at all, this one was probably, in relation to its contemporaries and predecessors, the best thing of the kind ever done—much better than the primers of Mrs. Fawcett or Jevons or any of its many successors. Moreover, the latter part of Book III. on Trade Combinations, Trade Unions, Trade Disputes, and Co-operation was the first satisfactory treatment on modern lines of these important topics.

After this volume [2] was out of the way, Marshall's health was at its worst. When in 1881 he went abroad to recuperate, his mind did not return to Money or to Foreign Trade, but was concentrated on the central theories which eventually appeared in the *Principles*.[3] Subject to the successive interruptions of his Oxford appointment, his removal to Cambridge, the preparation of his lectures there, his in-

[1] So much did the public like it that 15,000 copies had been sold before it was suppressed.

[2] Its preface mentioned a forthcoming companion volume on the "Economics of Trade and Finance," which was never written.

[3] Mrs. Marshall writes: "Book III. on Demand was largely thought out and written on the roof at Palermo, Nov. 1881–Feb. 1882."

cursion into the Bimetallic controversy and his Evidence before the Gold and Silver Commission, the next nine years were spent on the preparation of this book.

Marshall intended at first to cover the whole field of Economics in a single volume. His theory of Distribution was taking shape in 1883 and 1884.[1] In the summer of 1885 (in the Lakes), the first of his Cambridge Long Vacations, the volume began to assume its final form:

The work done during this year [he wrote][2] was not very satisfactory, partly because I was gradually outgrowing the older and narrower conception of my book, in which the abstract reasoning which forms the backbone of the science was to be made prominent, and had not yet mustered courage to commit myself straight off to a two-volume book which should be the chief product (as gradually improved) of my life's work.[3]

In 1886:

My chief work was recasting the plan of my book. This came to a head during my stay at Sheringham near

[1] It appears in outline in an article written in about two days in the summer of 1884, when he was staying at Rocquami Bay, Guernsey. This was published in the *Co-operative Annual* for 1885 under the title "Theories and Facts about Wages," and was reprinted in the same year as an appendix to his paper read before the Industrial Remuneration Conference.

[2] The following extracts are from some notes he put together summarising his work from 1885 to 1889.

[3] Also, "Work during the summer a good deal interrupted by making plans for my new house in Madingley Road."

Cromer in the summer. I then put the contents of my book into something like their final form, at least so far as the first volume is concerned. And thenceforward for the first time I began to try to put individual chapters into a form in which I expected them to be printed.

In 1887 (at Guernsey):

I did a great deal of writing at my book; and having arranged with Macmillan for its publication, I began just at the end of this academic year to send proofs to the printers: all of it except about half of Book VI. being typewritten in a form not ready for publication, but ready to be put into a form for publication—I mean the matter was nearly all there and the arrangement practically settled.

In 1888:

By the end of the Long Vacation I had got Book V. at the printer's, Book IV. being almost out of my hands. Later on I decided to bring before the Book on Normal Value or Distribution and Exchange a new Book on Cost of Production further considered,[1] putting into it (somewhat amplified) discussions which I had intended to keep for the later part of the Book on Normal Value. That Book now became Book VII. This decision was slowly reached, and not much further progress was made during this Calendar year.

In 1889:

During the first four months of 1889 I worked at Book VI., finishing the first draft of the first four

[1] After the first edition this Book was incorporated in Book V. So that *Value* again became Book VI.

chapters of it, and working off Book V. Meanwhile
I had paid a good deal of attention to the Mathematical
Appendix and got a good part of that into print. The
Long Vacation, of which eight weeks were spent at
Bordeaux Harbour, was occupied chiefly with Book VI.
chaps. v. and vi., and Book VII. chaps. i.-v.

The work was now pushed rapidly to a conclusion and was published in July 1890.

By 1890 Marshall's fame stood high,[1] and
the *Principles of Economics*,[2] Vol. I.,[3] was delivered into an expectant world. Its success
was immediate and complete. The book was
the subject of leading articles and full-dress
reviews throughout the Press. The journalists
could not distinguish the precise contributions
and innovations which it contributed to science;
but they discerned with remarkable quickness
that it ushered in a new age of economic thought.

[1] "Rarely in modern times," said the *Scotsman*, "has a man
achieved such a high reputation as an authority on such a slender
basis of published work."

[2] This was the first book in England to be published at a *net*
price, which gives it an important place in the history of the
publishing trade. (See Sir F. Macmillan's *The Net Book Agreement*,
1899, pp. 14-16.) It has been a remarkable example of sustained
circulation. In the first thirty years of its life 27,000 copies were
sold, being throughout at an almost steady rate of 1000 copies
a year, excluding the war. During the next ten years 20,000
copies were sold, *i.e.* at the rate of 2000 copies a year. The total
number printed up to the present time (end of 1932) is 57,000.

[3] The suffix Vol. I. was not dropped until the sixth edition in
1910.

"It is a great thing," said the *Pall Mall Gazette*, "to have a Professor at one of our old Universities devoting the work of his life to recasting the science of Political Economy as the Science of Social Perfectibility." The New Political Economy had arrived, and the Old Political Economy, the dismal science, "which treated the individual man as a purely selfish and acquisitive animal, and the State as a mere conglomeration of such animals," had passed away.[1] "It will serve," said the *Daily Chronicle*, "to restore the shaken credit of political economy, and will probably become for the present generation what Mill's *Principles* was for the last." "It has made almost all other accounts of the science antiquated or obsolete," said the *Manchester Guardian*. "It is not premature to predict that Professor Marshall's treatise will form a landmark in the development of political economy, and that its influence on the direction and temper of economic inquiries will be wholly good." These are samples from a general chorus.

It is difficult for those of us who have been brought up entirely under the influences of Marshall and his book to appreciate the position

---

[1] Not that Old P. E. was really thus, but this was the journalists' way of expressing the effect which Marshall's outlook made on them.

of the science in the long interregnum between Mill's *Principles of Political Economy* and Marshall's *Principles of Economics*, or to define just what difference was made by the publication of the latter. The following is an attempt, with help from notes supplied by Professor Edgeworth, to indicate some of its more striking contributions to knowledge.[1]

(1) The unnecessary controversy, caused by the obscurity of Ricardo and the rebound of Jevons, about the respective parts played by Demand and by Cost of Production in the determination of Value was finally cleared up. After Marshall's analysis there was nothing more to be said.

The new light thrown on Cost of Production [Prof. Edgeworth writes] enabled one more clearly to discern the great part which it plays in the determination of value; that the classical authors had been rightly guided by their intuitions, as Marshall has somewhere said, when they emphasised the forces of Supply above those of Demand. The rehabilitation of the older writers—much depreciated by Jevons, Böhm-Bawerk and others

---

[1] Including hints and anticipations in earlier writings; as Professor Edgeworth wrote, reviewing the first edition of the *Principles* (*The Academy*, August 30, 1890): "Some of Professor Marshall's leading ideas have been more or less fully expressed in his earlier book (the little *Economics of Industry*), and in certain papers which, though unpublished, have not been unknown. The light of dawn was diffused before the orb of day appeared above the horizon."

in the seventies and eighties of last century—produced on the reviewer of the first edition an impression which is thus expressed: "The mists of ephemeral criticism are dispelled. The eternal mountains reappear in their natural sublimity, contemplated from a kindred height."

(2) The general idea, underlying the proposition that Value is determined at the equilibrium point of Demand and Supply, was extended so as to discover a whole Copernican system, by which all the elements of the economic universe are kept in their places by mutual counterpoise and interaction.[1] The general theory of economic equilibrium was strengthened and made effective as an organon of thought by two powerful subsidiary conceptions—*the Margin* and *Substitution*. The notion of the Margin was extended beyond Utility to describe the equilibrium point in given conditions of any economic factor which can be regarded as capable of small variations about a given value, or in its functional relation to a given value. The notion of Substitution was introduced to describe the process by which Equilibrium is restored or brought about. In particular the

[1] Already in 1872, in his review of Jevons, Marshall was in possession of the idea of the mutually dependent positions of the economic factors. "Just as the motion of every body in the solar system," he there wrote, "affects and is affected by the motion of every other, so it is with the elements of the problem of political economy."

idea of *Substitution at the Margin*, not only between alternative objects of consumption, but also between the factors of production, was extraordinarily fruitful in results. Further, there is

the double relation in which the various agents of production stand to one another. On the one hand, they are often rivals for employment; any one that is more efficient than another in proportion to its cost tending to be substituted for it, and thus limiting the demand price for the other. And on the other hand, they all constitute the field of employment for each other; there is no field of employment for any one, except in so far as it is provided by the others: the national dividend which is the joint product of all, and which increases with the supply of each of them, is also the sole source of demand for each of them.[1]

This method allowed the subsumption of wages and profits under the general laws of value, supply and demand—just as previously the theory of money had been so subsumed. At the same time the peculiarities in the action of demand and supply which determine the wages of the labourer or the profits of the employer were fully analysed.

(3) The explicit introduction of the element of Time as a factor in economic analysis is mainly due to Marshall. The conceptions

[1] *Principles*, bk. vi. chap. xi. § 5.

of the "long" and "short" period are his, and one of his objects was to trace "a continuous thread running through and connecting the applications of the general theory of equilibrium of demand and supply to different periods of time." [1] Connected with these there are further distinctions, which we now reckon essential to clear thinking, which are first explicit in Marshall—particularly those between "external" and "internal" economies [2] and between "prime" and "supplementary" cost. Of these pairs the first was, I think, a complete novelty when the *Principles* appeared; the latter, however, already existed in the vocabulary of manufacture if not in that of economic analysis.

By means of the distinction between the long and the short period, the meaning of "normal" value was made precise; and with the aid of two further characteristically Marshallian conceptions—Quasi-Rent and the Representative Firm—the doctrine of Normal Profit was evolved.

All these are path-breaking ideas which no one who wants to think clearly can do without. Nevertheless, this is the quarter in which, in my opinion, the Marshall analysis is least com-

[1] *Principles,* bk. vi. chap. xi. § 1.

[2] The vital importance of this distinction to a correct theory of Equilibrium under conditions of increasing return is, of course, now obvious. But it was not so before the *Principles.*

plete and satisfactory, and where there remains
most to do. As he says himself in the Preface
to the first edition of the *Principles*, the element
of time "is the centre of the chief difficulty of
almost every economic problem."

(4) The special conception of Consumers'
Rent or Surplus, which was a natural development of Jevonian ideas, has perhaps proved less
fruitful of practical results than seemed likely at
first.[1] But one could not do without it as part
of the apparatus of thought, and it is particularly
important in the *Principles* because of the use
of it (in Professor Edgeworth's words) "to show
that *laissez-faire*, the maximum of advantage
attained by unrestricted competition, is not
necessarily the greatest possible advantage
attainable." Marshall's proof that *laissez-faire*
breaks down in certain conditions *theoretically*,
and not merely practically, regarded as a principle of maximum social advantage, was of great
philosophical importance. But Marshall does
not carry this particular argument very far,[2]

[1] Nevertheless, Professor Edgeworth points out, even "before
the publication of the *Principles* Marshall quite understood—what
the critics of the doctrine in question have not generally understood, and even some of the defenders have not adequately
emphasised—that the said measurement applies accurately only to
transactions which are on such a scale as not to disturb the
marginal value of money."

[2] *Industry and Trade*, however, is partly devoted to illustrating
it. "The present volume," he says in the Preface to that book,

and the further exploration of that field has been left to Marshall's favourite pupil and successor, Professor Pigou, who has shown in it what a powerful engine for cutting a way in tangled and difficult country the Marshall analysis affords in the hands of one who has been brought up to understand it well.

(5) Marshall's analysis of Monopoly should also be mentioned in this place; and perhaps his analysis of increasing return, especially where external economies exist, belongs better here than where I have mentioned it above.

Marshall's theoretical conclusions in this field and his strong sympathy with socialistic ideas were compatible, however, with an old-fashioned belief in the strength of the forces of competition. Professor Edgeworth writes:

I may record the strong impression produced on me the first time I met Marshall—far back in the eighties, I think—by his strong expression of the conviction that Competition would for many a long day rule the roast as a main determinant of value. Those were not his words, but they were of a piece with the dictum in his

"is in the main occupied with the influences which still make for sectional and class selfishness: with the limited tendencies of self-interest to direct each individual's action on those lines, in which it will be most beneficial to others; and with the still surviving tendencies of associated action by capitalists and other business men, as well as by employees, to regulate output, and action generally, by a desire for sectional rather than national advantage."

article on "The Old Generation of Economists and the New":[1] "When one person is willing to sell a thing at a price which another is willing to pay for it, the two manage to come together in spite of prohibitions of King or Parliament or of the officials of a Trust or Trade-Union."

(6) In the provision of terminology and apparatus to aid thought I do not think that Marshall did economists any greater service than by the explicit introduction of the idea of "elasticity." Book III. chap. iii. of the first edition of the *Principles*, which introduces the definition of "Elasticity of Demand,"[2] is virtually the earliest treatment[3] of a conception without the aid of which the advanced theory of Value and Distribution can scarcely make progress. The notion that demand may respond to a change of price to an extent that may be either more or less than in proportion

---

[1] *Quarterly Journal of Economics*, 1896, vol. xi. p. 129.

[2] Supplemented by the mathematical note in the Appendix.

[3] Strictly, the earliest reference to "elasticity" is to be found in Marshall's contribution "On the Graphic Method of Statistics" to the Jubilee Volume of the *Royal Statistical Society* (1885), p. 260. But it is introduced there only in a brief concluding note, and mainly with the object of showing that a simple diagrammatic measure of elasticity is furnished by the ratio between the two sections into which that part of the tangent to the demand curve which lies between the axes is divided by the point of contact. Mrs. Marshall tells me that he hit on the notion of elasticity as he sat on the roof at Palermo shaded by the bath-cover in 1881, and was highly delighted with it.

had been, of course, familiar since the discussions at the beginning of the nineteenth century about the relation between the supply and the price of wheat.[1]   Indeed, it is rather remarkable that the notion was not more clearly disentangled either by Mill or by Jevons.[2]   But it was so.   And the concept $e = \dfrac{dx}{x} \div -\dfrac{dy}{y}$ is wholly Marshall's.

The way in which Marshall introduces Elasticity, without any suggestion that the idea is novel, is remarkable and characteristic.   The field of investigation opened up by this instrument of thought is again one where the full fruits have been reaped by Professor Pigou rather than by Marshall himself.

(7) The historical introduction to the *Prin-*

[1] Mill quotes Tooke's *History of Prices* in this connection.

[2] Professor Edgeworth in his article on "Elasticity" in Palgrave's *Dictionary* refers particularly to Mill's *Political Economy*, bk. iii. chap. ii. § 4, and chap. viii. § 2, as representative of the pre-Marshall treatment of the matter.   The first of these passages points out the varying proportions in which demand may respond to variations of price;   the second treats (in effect) of the unitary elasticity of the demand for money.   Professor Edgeworth now adds a reference to bk. iii. chap. xviii. § 5, where Mill deals in substance with the effect of elasticity on the Equation of International Demand.   Elsewhere in this chapter Mill speaks of a demand being "more extensible by cheapness" (§ 4) and of the "extensibility of their [foreign countries'] demand for its [the home country's] commodities" (§ 8).

ciples deserves some comment.   In the first edition, Book I. includes two chapters entitled "The Growth of Free Industry and Enterprise." In the latest editions most of what has been retained out of these chapters has been relegated to an Appendix.   Marshall was always in two minds about this.   On the one hand, his views as to the perpetually changing character of the subject-matter of Economics led him to attach great importance to the historical background as a corrective to the idea that the axioms of to-day are permanent.   He was also dissatisfied with the learned but half-muddled work of the German historical school.   On the other hand, he was afraid of spending too much time on these matters (at one period he had embarked on historical inquiries on a scale which, he said, would have occupied six volumes), and of over-loading with them the essential matter of his book.   At the time when he was occupied with economic history there was very little ready-made material to go upon, and he probably wasted much strength straying unnecessarily along historical by-ways and vacillating as to the importance to be given in his own book to the historical background.   The resulting com-promise, as realised in the *Principles*, was not very satisfactory.   Everything is boiled down into wide generalisations, the evidence for which he has not space to display.[1] Marshall's best historical work is to be found, perhaps, in *Industry and Trade*, published in 1919, many years after most of the work had been done. The historical passages of the *Principles* were brusquely assailed by Dr. William Cunningham in an address before the Royal Historical Society, printed in the *Economic Journal*, vol. ii. (1892); and Marshall, breaking his general rule of not replying to criticism, came successfully out of the controversy in a reply printed in the same issue of the *Journal*.[2]

The way in which Marshall's *Principles of Economics* is written is more unusual than the

---

[1] Marshall himself wrote (in his reply to Dr. Cunningham, *Economic Journal*, vol. ii. p. 507): "I once proposed to write a treatise on economic history, and for many years I collected materials for it. Afterwards I selected such part of these as helped to explain why many of the present conditions and problems of industry are only of recent date, and worked it into the chapters in question. But they took up much more space than could be spared for them. So I recast and compressed them; and in the process they lost, no doubt, some sharpness of outline and particularity of statement."

[2] Dr. Clapham writes: "In reading the Appendices to *Industry and Trade* I was very much impressed with Marshall's knowledge of economic history since the seventeenth century, as it was known thirty years ago, *i.e.* at the time of the controversy. I feel sure that at that time he understood the seventeenth to nineteenth centuries better than Cunningham, and he had—naturally—a feeling for their quantitative treatment to which Cunningham never attained."

casual reader will notice. It is elaborately un-
sensational and under-emphatic. Its rhetoric
is of the simplest, most unadorned order. It
flows in a steady, lucid stream, with few
passages which stop or perplex the intelligent
reader, even though he know but little economics. Claims to novelty or to originality on
the part of the author himself are altogether
absent.[1] Passages imputing error to others are
rare, and it is explained that earlier writers of
repute must be held to have *meant* what is right
and reasonable, whatever they may have said.[2]

[1] As one intelligent reviewer remarked (*The Guardian*, October
15, 1890): "This book has two aspects. On the one hand, it is
an honest and obstinate endeavour to find out the truth; on the
other hand, it is an ingenious attempt to disclaim any credit for
discovering it, on the ground that it was all implicitly contained
in the works of earlier writers, especially Ricardo." But most of
them were taken in. The following is typical (*Daily Chronicle*,
July 24, 1890): "Mr. Marshall makes no affectation of new discoveries or new departures; he professes merely to give a modern
version of the old doctrines adjusted to the results of more recent
investigation."

[2] Marshall carried this rather too far. But it was an essential
truth to which he held firmly, that those individuals who are
endowed with a special genius for the subject and have a powerful
economic intuition will often be more right in their conclusions
and implicit presumptions than in their explanations and explicit
statements. That is to say, their intuitions will be in advance of
their analysis and their terminology. Great respect, therefore, is
due to their general scheme of thought, and it is a poor thing to
pester their memories with criticism which is really verbal.
Marshall's own economic intuition was extraordinary, and lenience
towards the apparent errors of great predecessors is treatment to
which in future times he will himself have an exceptional claim.

The connexity and continuity of the economic elements, as signified in Marshall's two mottoes, "Natura non facit saltum" and "The many in the one, the one in the many," are the chief grounds of difficulty. But, subject to this, the chief impression which the book makes on the minds of uninitiated readers—particularly on those who do not get beyond Book IV.—is apt to be that they are perusing a clear, apt, and humane exposition of fairly obvious matters.

By this stylistic achievement Marshall attained some of his objects. The book reached the general public. It increased the public esteem of Economics. The minimum of controversy was provoked. The average reviewer liked the author's attitude to his subject-matter, to his predecessors, and to his readers, and delighted Marshall by calling attention to the proper stress laid by him on the ethical element and to the much required humanising which the dismal science received at his hands;[1] and, at the same time, could remain happily insensible to the book's intellectual stature. As time has gone on, moreover, the intellectual qualities of the

[1] Fashions change! When, nearly thirty years later, *Industry and Trade* appeared, one reviewer wrote (*Athenaeum*, October 31, 1919): "Perhaps its least satisfactory feature is its moral tone. Not because that tone is low—quite the contrary; but because, in a scientific treatise, a moral tone, however elevated, seems altogether out of place."

book have permeated English economic thought, without noise or disturbance, in a degree which can easily be overlooked.

The method has, on the other hand, serious disadvantages. The lack of emphasis and of strong light and shade, the sedulous rubbing away of rough edges and salients and projections, until what is most novel can appear as trite, allows the reader to pass too easily through. Like a duck leaving water, he can escape from this douche of ideas with scarce a wetting. The difficulties are concealed; the most ticklish problems are solved in footnotes; a pregnant and original judgement is dressed up as a platitude. The author furnishes his ideas with no labels of salesmanship and few hooks for them to hang by in the wardrobe of the mind. A student can read the *Principles*, be fascinated by its pervading charm, think that he comprehends it, and yet, a week later, know but little about it. How often has it not happened even to those who have been brought up on the *Principles*, lighting upon what seems a new problem or a new solution, to go back to it and to find, after all, that the problem and a better solution have been always there, yet quite escaping notice! It needs much study and independent thought on the reader's own part before he can know the half of what is contained

in the concealed crevices of that rounded globe
of knowledge which is Marshall's *Principles of
Economics*.

VII

The Marshalls returned in 1885 to the Cambridge of the early years after the reforms which
finally removed restrictions upon the marriage
of Fellows.   They built for themselves a small
house, called Balliol Croft, on St. John's College
land in the Madingley Road, close to the Backs,
yet just on the outskirts of the town, so that
on one side open country stretched towards
Madingley Hill.   Here Alfred Marshall lived
for nearly forty years.   The house, built in a
sufficient garden, on an unconventional plan so
as to get as much light as possible, just accom-
modated the two of them and a faithful maid.
His study, lined with books, and filled trans-
versally with shelves, had space by the fire for
two chairs.   Here were held his innumerable
tête-à-tête with pupils, who would be furnished
as the afternoon wore on with a cup of tea and
a slice of cake on an adjacent stool or shelf.
Larger gatherings took place downstairs, where
the dining-room and Mrs. Marshall's sitting-
room could be thrown into one on the occasion
of entertainments.   The unvarying character
of the surroundings—upstairs the books and

nests of drawers containing manuscript, down-stairs the Michelangelo figures from the Sistine Chapel let into the furniture, and at the door the face of Sarah the maid,[1] had a charm and fascination for those who paid visits to their Master year after year, like the Cell or Oratory of a Sage.

In that first age of married society in Cambridge, when the narrow circle of the spouses-regnant of the Heads of Colleges and of a few wives of Professors was first extended, several of the most notable Dons, particularly in the School of Moral Science, married students of Newnham. The double link between husbands and between wives bound together a small cultured society of great simplicity and distinction. This circle was at its full strength in my boyhood, and, when I was first old enough to be asked out to luncheon or to dinner, it was to these houses that I went. I remember a homely, intellectual atmosphere which it is harder to find in the swollen, heterogeneous Cambridge of to-day. The entertainments at

---

[1] She lived with them for more than forty years on terms almost of intimacy. Marshall would often extol her judgement and wisdom. He himself designed the small kitchen, like a ship's cabin, in which she dwelt at Balliol Croft. Here Jowett, when he was staying with the Marshalls, visited Sarah to discuss her religious difficulties. Marshall was much loved by his servants and College gyps. He treated them like human beings and talked to them about the things in which he was interested himself.

the Marshalls' were generally occasioned, in later days, by the visit of some fellow-economist, often an eminent foreigner, and the small luncheon party would usually include a couple of undergraduates and a student or young lecturer from Newnham. I particularly remember meeting in this way Adolf Wagner and N. G. Pierson, representatives of a generation of economists which is now almost past. Marshall did not much care about going to other people's houses, and was at his best fitting his guests comfortably into a narrow space, calling out staff directions to his wife, in unembarrassed, half - embarrassed mood, with laughing, high-pitched voice and habitual jokes and phrases. He had great conversational powers on all manner of matters; his cheerfulness and gaiety were unbroken; and, in the presence of his bright eyes and smiling talk and unaffected absurdity, no one could feel dull.

In earlier days, particularly between 1885 and 1900, he was fond of asking working-men leaders to spend a week-end with him—for example, Thomas Burt, Ben Tillett, Tom Mann, and many others. Sometimes these visits would be fitted in with meetings of the Social Discussion Society, which the visitor would address. In this way he came to know most of the leading co-operators and Trade Unionists

of the past generation.   In truth, he sympathised
with the Labour Movement and with Socialism
(just as J. S. Mill had) in every way except intellectually.[1]

Marshall was now settled in an environment
and in habits which were not to be changed, and
we must record in rapid survey the outward
events of his life from 1885 to the resignation
of his professorship in 1908.

From 1885 to 1890 he was mainly occupied,
as we have seen, with the *Principles*.   But his
other activities included, particularly, his paper
before the Industrial Remuneration Conference

---

[1] In the Preface to *Industry and Trade* he wrote: "For more
than a decade, I remained under the conviction that the suggestions, which are associated with the word 'socialism,' were the
most important subject of study, if not in the world, yet at all
events for me.   But the writings of socialists generally repelled me,
almost as much as they attracted me; because they seemed far
out of touch with realities: and, partly for that reason, I decided
to say little on the matter, till I had thought much longer.   Now,
when old age indicates that my time for thought and speech is
nearly ended, I see on all sides marvellous developments of working-class faculty: and, partly in consequence, a broader and
firmer foundation for socialistic schemes than when Mill wrote.
But no socialistic scheme, yet advanced, seems to make adequate
provision for the maintenance of high enterprise and individual
strength of character; nor to promise a sufficiently rapid increase
in the business plant and other material implements of production.
. . . It has seemed to me that those have made most real progress
towards the distant goal of ideally perfect social organisation, who
have concentrated their energies on some particular difficulties in
the way, and not spent strength on endeavouring to rush past
them."

in 1885, his evidence before the Gold and Silver Commission in 1887–88, and his Presidential Address before the Co-operative Congress in 1889. In the summer of 1890 he delivered his interesting Presidential Address on "Some Aspects of Competition" to the Economic Section of the British Association at Leeds. He was also much occupied with his lectures, and these five years were the most active and productive of his life.

He gave two lectures a week in a general course, and one lecture a week on special theoretical difficulties; but he lectured, as a rule, in only two terms out of three, making about forty-five lectures in the year. Two afternoons a week, from four to seven, Professor Marshall, it was announced, "will be at home to give advice and assistance to any members of the University who may call on him, whether they are attending his lectures or not." In the late eighties the attendance at his general courses would vary between forty and seventy, and at his special courses half that number. But his methods choked off—more or less deliberately—the less serious students, and as the academic year progressed the attendance would fall to the lower figure.

It was not Marshall's practice to write out his lectures.

He rarely used notes [Mrs. Marshall writes] except for lectures on Economic History. He sometimes made a few notes before he went to lecture, and thought over them on his way to the class. He said that the reason why he had so many pupils who thought for themselves was that he never cared to present the subject in an orderly and systematic form or to give information. What he cared to do in lectures was to make the students *think with him.* He gave questions once a week on a part of the subject which he had not lectured over, and then answered the questions in class. He took immense pains in looking over the answers, and used red ink on them freely.[1]

I think that the informality of his lectures may have increased as time went on. Certainly in 1906, when I attended them, it was impossible to bring away coherent notes. But the above was always his general method. His lectures were not, like Sidgwick's, books in the making. This practice may have contributed, incidentally, to the retardation of his published work. But the sharp distinction which he favoured between instruction by book and oral instruction by lecture was, as he developed it, extraordinarily stimulating for the better men and where the class was not too large. It is a difficult method to employ where the class exceeds forty at the most (my memory of the size of his class when

[1] I have papers which I wrote for him on which his red-ink comments and criticisms occupy almost as much space as my answers.

I attended it is of nearer twenty than forty), and it is not suited to students who have no real aptitude or inclination for economics (in whose interest the curricula of the vast Economic Schools of to-day are mainly designed). The following titles of successive courses, soon after he arrived in Cambridge, indicate the ground which he purported to cover:

1885–86. October Term: Foreign Trade and Money.

Easter „ : Speculation, Taxation, etc. (Mill, IV. and V.).

1886–87. October „ : Production and Value.

Lent „ : Distribution.

After the publication of the *Principles* in 1890, his first task was to prepare the abridgement, entitled *Economics of Industry*,[1] which appeared early in 1892.[2] He also spent much

---

[1] This book has been frequently reprinted, and revised editions were prepared in 1896 and 1899. 108,000 copies of it have been printed up to date (end of 1932). The book has sold at a steady rate of about 2500 copies a year since it first came out, and after a life of forty years is still maintaining the same rate. In conjunction with the sale of the *Principles* (*vide* p. 220, above), this is a measure of the overwhelming influence which Marshall has exercised over economic education for nearly half a century.

[2] The concluding chapter on "Trade Unions" goes outside the field of the *Principles* and incorporates some material from the earlier *Economics of Industry*.

R

time on the successive revisions of the *Principles*, the most important changes being introduced in the third edition, published in 1895, and the fifth edition in 1907. It is doubtful whether the degree of improvement effected corresponded to the labour involved. These revisions were a great obstacle to his getting on with what was originally intended to be volume ii. of the *Principles*.

The main interruption, however, came from his membership of the Royal Commission on Labour, 1891–94. He welcomed greatly this opportunity of getting into close touch with the raw material of his subject, and he played a big part in the drafting of the Final Report. The parts dealing with Trade Unions, Minimum Wage, and Irregularity of Employment were especially his work.

Meanwhile he was at work on the continuation of the *Principles*.

But he wasted a great deal of time [Mrs. Marshall writes] because he changed his method of treatment so often. In 1894 he began a historical treatment, which he called later on a White Elephant, because it was on such a large scale that it would have taken many volumes to complete. Later on he used fragments of the White Elephant in the descriptive parts of *Industry and Trade*.

Marshall's work on the Labour Commission was only one of a series of services to Governmental inquiries. In 1893 he gave evidence before the Royal Commission on the Aged Poor, in which he proposed to associate Charity Organisation Committees with the administration of the Poor Law. Early in 1899 he gave carefully prepared evidence before the Indian Currency Committee. His evidence on monetary theory was in part a repetition of what he had said to the Gold and Silver Commission eleven years earlier, but he himself considered that the new version was an improvement and constituted his best account of the theory of money. The parts dealing with specifically Indian problems were supported by many statistical diagrams. His interest in the economic and currency problems of India had been first aroused during the time at Oxford when it was his duty to lecture to Indian Civil Service Probationers. He was pleased with his detailed realistic inquiries into Indian problems,[1] and the great rolls of Indian charts, not all of which were published, were always at hand as part of the furniture of his study.

Later in the same year, 1899, he prepared Memoranda on the Classification and Incidence of Imperial and Local Taxes for the Royal Commission on Local Taxation. In 1903, at the height of the Tariff Reform controversy, he

[1] He had many devoted Indian (and also Japanese) pupils.

wrote, at the request of the Treasury, his admirable Memorandum on "The Fiscal Policy of International Trade." This was printed in 1908 as a Parliamentary paper at the instance of Mr. Lloyd George, then Chancellor of the Exchequer, "substantially as it was written originally." The delay of a critical five years in the date of publication was characteristically explained by Marshall as follows:

Some large corrections of, and additions to, this Memorandum were lost in the post abroad [1] in August 1903; and when I re-read the uncorrected proofs of it in the autumn, I was so dissatisfied with it that I did not avail myself of the permission kindly given to me to publish it independently. The haste with which it was written and its brevity are partly responsible for its lack of arrangement, and for its frequent expression almost dogmatically of private opinion, where careful argument would be more in place. It offends against my rule to avoid controversial matters; and, instead of endeavouring to probe to the causes of causes, as a student's work should, it is concerned mainly with proximate causes and their effects. I elected, therefore, to remain silent on the fiscal issue until I could incorporate what I had to say about it in a more careful and fuller discussion; and I am now engaged on that task. But it proceeds slowly; and time flies.

Marshall's growing inhibitions are exposed in

[1] They were stolen by a local post-mistress in the Tyrol for the sake of the stamps on the envelope.

these sentences. The difficulties of bringing him to the point of delivering up his mind's possessions were getting almost insuperable. In 1908 he resigned his professorship, in the hope that release from the heavy duties of lecturing and teaching might expedite matters.

VIII

During his twenty-three years as Professor he took part in three important movements, which deserve separate mention—the foundation of the British Economic Association (now the Royal Economic Society), the Women's Degrees Controversy at Cambridge, and the establishment of the Cambridge Economics Tripos.

1. The circular entitled "Proposal to Form an English Economic Association," which was the first public step towards the establishment of the Royal Economic Society, was issued on October 24, 1890, over the sole signature of Alfred Marshall, though, of course, with the co-operation of others.[1] It invited all lecturers on Economics in any University or public College in the United Kingdom, the members of the Councils

[1] Marshall signed, I think, primarily in his capacity as President of the Economics Section of the British Association for 1890, at that year's meeting of which the need for the establishment of an Economic journal had been strongly urged.

of the London, Dublin, and Manchester Statistical Societies, and the members of the London Political Economy Club, together with a few other persons, including members of the Committee of Section F of the British Association, to attend a private meeting at University College, London, on November 20, 1890, under the Chairmanship of Lord Goschen, the Chancellor of the Exchequer, "to discuss proposals for the foundation of an Economic Society or Association, and, in conjunction therewith, of an Economic journal." This initial circular letter lays down the general lines which the Society has actually pursued during the subsequent years of its existence.[1] The only vocal dissentient

---

[1] The chief difference of opinion, discovered at the outset, regarding the Society's scope, was indicated as follows: "Almost the only question on which a difference of opinion has so far shown itself is whether or not the Association should be open to all those who are sufficiently interested in Economics to be willing to subscribe to its funds. . . . There are some who think that the general lines to be followed should be those of an English 'learned Society,' while others would prefer those of the American Economic Association, which holds meetings only at rare intervals, and the membership of which does not profess to confer any sort of diploma." At the meeting a resolution was carried unanimously, proposed by Mr. Courtney and supported by Professor Sidgwick and Professor Edgeworth, "that any person who desires to further the aims of the Association, and is approved by the Council, be admitted to membership." The wording of the Society's constitution shows some traces of compromise between the two ideas, but in practice the precedent of the American Economic Association has always been followed.

was Mr. G. Bernard Shaw,[1] who, whilst approving everything else, suggested, "with all respect to Mr. Goschen, that the head of the Association should not be a gentleman who was identified with any political party in the State."

2. The controversy about admitting women to degrees, which tore Cambridge in two in 1896, found Marshall in the camp which was opposed to the women's claims. He had been in closest touch with Newnham since its foundation, through his wife and through the Sidgwicks. When he went to Bristol he had been, in his own words, "attracted thither chiefly by the fact that it was the first College in England to open its doors freely to women." A considerable proportion of his pupils had been women. In his first printed essay (on "The Future of the Working Classes," in 1873) the opening passage is an eloquent claim, in sympathy with Mill, for the emancipation of

[1] Mr. Bernard Shaw read a paper before the Economics Section of the British Association in 1888, remarking, as Mr. L. L. Price (who was then secretary) relates, that his promotion from the street corner to read a paper to a learned body was a sign of the times. It was of this occasion that Sidgwick wrote: "The Committee had invited a live Socialist, red-hot 'from the streets,' as he told us, who sketched in a really brilliant address the rapid series of steps by which modern society is to pass peacefully into social democracy. There was a peroration rhetorically effective as well as daring. Altogether a noteworthy performance—the man's name is Bernard Shaw. Myers says he has written books worth reading" (*Henry Sidgwick: a Memoir*, p. 497).

women. All Mill's instances "tend to show," he says in that paper, "how our progress could be accelerated if we would unwrap the swaddling-clothes in which artificial customs have enfolded woman's mind and would give her free scope womanfully to discharge her duties to the world." Marshall's attitude, therefore, was a sad blow to his own little circle, and, being exploited by the other side, it played some part in the overwhelming defeat which the reformers eventually suffered. In his taking this course Marshall's intellect could find excellent reasons. Indeed, the lengthy fly-sheet, which he circulated to members of the Senate, presents, in temperate and courteous terms, a brilliant and perhaps convincing case against the complete assimilation of women's education to that of men. Nevertheless, a congenital bias, which by a man's fifty-fourth year of life has gathered secret strength, may have played a bigger part in the conclusion than the obedient intellect.

3. Lastly, there are Marshall's services in the foundation of the Cambridge School of Economics.

When Marshall came back to Cambridge in 1885, papers on Political Economy were included both in the Moral Sciences Tripos and in the History Tripos.[1] The separate founda-

[1] At Marshall's lectures in the later eighties, apart from students

tion of these two schools some twenty years earlier had worked a great revolution in liberalising the studies of the University.[1] But, almost as soon as he was Professor, Marshall felt strongly that the time had come for a further step forward; and he particularly disliked the implication of the existing curriculum, that Economics was the sort of subject which could be satisfactorily undertaken as a subsidiary study. Immediately that he was back in Cambridge in 1885 he was in rebellion against the idea that his lectures must be adapted to the requirements of an examination of which Economics formed but a part.[2] His Inaugural Lecture constituted, in effect, a demand that

from other departments and B.A.'s who might be attracted out of curiosity about the subject, there would be a dozen or less Moral Science students and two dozen or less History students.

[1] Marshall summarised the history of the matter as follows in his *Plea for the Creation of a Curriculum in Economics* (1902): "In foreign countries economics has always been closely associated with history or law, or political science, or some combination of these studies. The first (Cambridge) Moral Sciences Examination (1851–1860) included ethics, law, history, and economics; but not mental science or logic. In 1860, however, philosophy and logic were introduced and associated with ethics; while history and political philosophy, jurisprudence and political economy formed an alternative group. In 1867 provision was made elsewhere for law and history; and mental science and logic have since then struck the keynote of the Moral Sciences Tripos."

[2] For his contentions with Sidgwick about this (and for a characteristic specimen of Sidgwick's delightful and half-humorous reaction to criticism) see *Henry Sidgwick: a Memoir*, p. 394.

Economics should have a new status; and it was so interpreted by Sidgwick. The following declaration from that Lecture is of some historical importance as almost the first blow in the struggle for the independent status which Economics has now won almost everywhere:

There is wanted wider and more scientific knowledge of facts: an organon stronger and more complete, more able to analyse and help in the solution of the economic problems of the age. To develop and apply the organon rightly is our most urgent need; and this requires all the faculties of a trained scientific mind. Eloquence and erudition have been lavishly spent in the service of Economics. They are good in their way; but what is most wanted now is the power of keeping the head cool and clear in tracing and analysing the combined action of many combined causes. Exceptional genius being left out of account, this power is rarely found save amongst those who have gone through a severe course of work in the more advanced sciences. Cambridge has more such men than any other University in the world. But, alas! few of them turn to the task. Partly this is because the only curriculum in which Economics has a very important part to play is that of the Moral Sciences Tripos. And many of those who are fitted for the highest and hardest economic work are not attracted by the metaphysical studies that lie at the threshold of that Tripos.

This claim of Marshall's corresponded to the conception of the subject which dominated his own work. Marshall was the first great

economist *pur sang* that there ever was; the first
who devoted his life to building up the subject
as a separate science, standing on its own
foundations, with as high standards of scientific
accuracy as the physical or the biological
sciences. It was Marshall who finally saw to
it that "never again will a Mrs. Trimmer, a
Mrs. Marcet, or a Miss Martineau earn a
goodly reputation by throwing economic principles into the form of a catechism or of simple
tales, by aid of which any intelligent governess
might make clear to the children nestling
around her where lies economic truth." [1] But
—much more than this—after his time Economics could never be again one of a number of
subjects which a Moral Philosopher would take
in his stride, one Moral Science out of several,
as Mill, Jevons, and Sidgwick took it. He was
the first to take up this professional scientific
attitude to the subject, as something above and
outside current controversy, as far from politics
as physiology from the general practitioner.

As time went on Political Economy came to
occupy, in Part II. of the Moral Sciences Tripos,
a position nearer to Marshall's ideal. But he
was not satisfied until, in 1903, his victory was
complete by the establishment of a separate

[1] From his article "The Old Generation of Economists and the
New," *Quarterly Journal of Economics*, January 1897.

School and Tripos in Economics and associated branches of Political Science.[1]

Thus in a formal sense Marshall was Founder of the Cambridge School of Economics. Far more so was he its Founder in those informal relations with many generations of pupils, which played so great a part in his life's work and in determining the course of their lives' work.

To his colleagues Marshall might sometimes seem tiresome and obstinate; to the outside world he might appear pontifical or unpractical; but to his pupils he was, and remained, a true sage and master, outside criticism, one who was their father in the spirit and who gave them such inspiration and comfort as they drew from no other source. Those eccentricities and individual ways, which might stand between him and the world, became, for them, part of what they loved. They built up sagas round him (of which Mr. Fay is, perhaps, the chief repository), and were not content unless he were, without concession, his own unique self. The youth are not satisfied unless their Socrates is a little odd.

[1] Sidgwick had been finally converted to the idea in 1900, shortly before his death. Marshall's ideals of economic education are set forth in his "Plea for the Creation of a Curriculum in Economics" and his "Introduction to the Tripos in Economics. . . ."

It is difficult to describe on paper the effect he produced or his way of doing it. The pupil would come away with an extraordinary feeling that he was embarked on the most interesting and important voyage in the world. He would walk back along the Madingley Road, labouring under more books, which had been taken from the shelves for him as the interview went on, than he could well carry, convinced that here was a subject worthy of his life's study. Marshall's double nature, coming out informally and spontaneously, filled the pupil seated by him with a double illumination. The young man was presented with a standard of intellectual integrity, and with it a disinterestedness of purpose which satisfied him intellectually and morally at the same time. The subject itself had seemed to grow under the hands of master and pupil as they had talked. There were endless possibilities, not out of reach. "Everything was friendly and informal," Mr. Sanger has written of these occasions (*Nation*, July 19, 1924):

There was no pretence that economic science was a settled affair—like grammar or algebra—which had to be learnt, not criticised; it was treated as a subject in the course of development. When once Alfred Marshall gave a copy of his famous book to a pupil, inscribed "To ——, in the hope that in due course he will render this treatise obsolete," this was not a piece of mock modesty, but an insistence on his belief that economics was a growing science, that as yet nothing was to be considered as final.

It must not be supposed that Marshall was undiscriminating towards his pupils. He was highly critical and even sharp-tongued. He managed to be encouraging, whilst at the same time very much the reverse of flattering. Pupils, in after life, would send him their books with much trepidation as to what he would say or think. The following anecdote of his insight and quick observation when lecturing is told by Dr. Clapham: "You have two very interesting men from your College at my lecture," he said to a College Tutor. "When I come to a very stiff bit, A. B. says to himself, 'This is too hard for me: I won't try to grasp it.' C. D. tries to grasp it but fails"—Marshall's voice running off on to a high note and his face breaking up into his smile. It was an exact estimate of the two men's intelligences and tempers.

It is through his pupils, even more than his writings, that Marshall is the father of Economic Science as it exists in England to-day. So long ago as 1888, Professor Foxwell was able to write: "Half the economic chairs in the United Kingdom are occupied by his pupils, and the share taken by them in general economic instruc-

tion in England is even larger than this." [1]   To-
day, through pupils and the pupils of pupils, his
dominion is almost complete.   More than most
men he could, when the time came for him to go
away, repeat his *Nunc Dimittis*, on a comparison
of his achievement with the aim he had set
himself in the concluding sentence of his
Inaugural Lecture in 1885:

It will be my most cherished ambition, my highest
endeavour, to do what with my poor ability and my
limited strength I may, to increase the numbers of those
whom Cambridge, the great mother of strong men,[2]
sends out into the world with cool heads but warm
hearts, willing to give some at least of their best powers
to grappling with the social suffering around them; resolved not to rest content till they have done what in
them lies to discover how far it is possible to open up
to all the material means of a refined and noble life.

IX

Marshall retired from the Chair of Political
Economy at Cambridge in 1908, aged sixty-six.
He belonged to the period of small salaries and
no pensions.   Nevertheless, he had managed
out of his professorial stipend (of £700, including his fellowship), which he never augmented

---

[1] "The Economic Movement in England," *Quarterly Journal
of Economics*, vol. ii. p. 92.

[2] Dr. Jowett took strong exception to this phrase.

either by examining or by journalism,[1] to maintain at his own expense a small lending library for undergraduates, to found a triennial Essay Prize of the value of £60 [2] for the encouragement of original research, and privately to pay stipends of £100 a year to one, or sometimes two, young lecturers for whom the University made no provision and who could not have remained otherwise on the teaching staff of the School of Economics. At the same time, with the aid of receipts from the sales of his books,[3] he had saved just sufficient to make retirement financially possible. As it turned out, the receipts from his books became, after the publication of *Industry and Trade*, so considerable that, at the end of his life, he was better off than he had ever been; and he used to say, when Macmillan's annual cheque arrived, that he hardly knew what to do with the money. He left his Economic library to the University

[1] All his many services to the State were, of course, entirely unpaid.

[2] In 1913 he transferred to the University a sufficient capital sum to provide an equivalent income in perpetuity.

[3] He always insisted on charging a lower price for his books than was usual for works of a similar size and character. He was a reckless proof-corrector, and he kept matter in type for years before publication. Some portions of *Industry and Trade*, which he had by him in proof for fifteen years before publication, are said to constitute a "record." He never regarded books as income-producing objects, except by accident.

of Cambridge, and most of his estate and any future receipts from his copyrights are also to fall ultimately to the University for the encouragement of the study of Economics.

Freed from the labour of lecturing and from the responsibility for pupils,[1] he was now able to spend what time and strength were left him in a final effort to gather in the harvest of his prime. Eighteen years had passed since the publication of the *Principles*, and masses of material had accumulated for consolidation and compression into books. He had frequently changed his plans about the scope and content of his later volumes, and the amount of material to be handled exceeded his powers of co-ordination. In the preface to the fifth edition of the *Principles* (1907) he explains that in 1895 he had decided to arrange his material in three volumes: I. *Modern Conditions of Industry and Trade*; II. *Credit and Employment*; III. *The Economic Functions of Government*. By 1907 four volumes were becoming necessary. So he decided to concentrate upon two of them, namely: I. *National Industry and Trade*; and II. *Money, Credit and Employment*. This was the final plan, except that, as time went on,

---

[1] He still continued, up to the time of the war, to see students in the afternoons—though perhaps former pupils (by that time young dons) more than newcomers.

S

Employment was squeezed out of the second of these volumes in favour of International Trade or *Commerce*. Even so, twelve more years passed by before, in his seventy-seventh year, *Industry and Trade* was published.

During this period the interruptions to the main matter in hand were inconsiderable. He wrote occasional letters to *The Times*—on Mr. Lloyd George's Budget (1909), in controversy with Professor Karl Pearson on "Alcoholism and Efficiency" (1910), on "A Fight to a Finish" and "Civilians in Warfare" on the outbreak of war (1914), and on Premium Bonds (1919). He wrote to the *Economist* in 1916 urging increased taxation to defray the expenses of the war; and in 1917 he contributed a chapter on "National Taxation after the War" to *After-War Problems*, a volume edited by Mr. W. H. Dawson.

Marshall's letters to *The Times* on the outbreak of war are of some interest. When he was asked, before war was actually declared, to sign a statement that we ought not to go to war because we had no interest in the coming struggle, he replied: "I think the question of peace or war must turn on national duty as much as on our interest. I hold that we ought to mobilise instantly, and announce that we shall declare war if the Germans invade Belgium;

and everybody knows they will." For many years he had taken seriously Pan-Germanic ambitions, and he headed his letter "A Fight to a Finish." Thus he took up a definitely anti-pacifist attitude, and did not fluctuate from this as time went on. But he was much opposed to the inflaming of national passions. He remembered that he had "known and loved Germany," and that they were "a people exceptionally conscientious and upright."[1] He held, therefore, that "it is our interest as well as our duty to respect them and make clear that we desire their friendship, but yet to fight them with all our might." And he expressed "an anxiety lest popular lectures should inflame passions which will do little or nothing towards securing victory, but may very greatly increase the slaughter on both sides, which must be paid as the price of resisting Germany's aggressive tendencies." These sentiments brought down on him the wrath of the more savage patriots.

At last, in 1919, *Industry and Trade* appeared,

[1] "Those," he wrote to *The Times* on August 22, 1914, "who know and love Germany, even while revolted at the hectoring militarism which is more common there than here, should insist that we have no cause to scorn them, though we have good cause to fight them. . . . As a people I believe them to be exceptionally conscientious and upright, sensitive to the calls of duty, tender in their family affections, true and trusty in friendship. Therefore they are strong and to be feared, but not to be vilified."

a great effort of will and determination on the part of one who had long passed the age when most men rest from their labours.

It is altogether a different sort of book from the *Principles*. The most part of it is descriptive. A full third is historical and summarises the results of his long labours in that field. The co-ordination of the parts into a single volume is rather artificial. The difficulties of such co-ordination, which had beset him for so many years, are not really overcome. The book is not so much a structural unity as an opportunity for bringing together a number of partly related matters about which Marshall had something of value to say to the world. This is particularly the case with its sixteen Appendices, which are his device for bringing to birth a number of individual monographs or articles. Several of these had been written a great number of years before the book was issued. They were quite well suited to separate publication, and it must be judged a fault in him that they were hoarded as they were.

The three books into which the volume is divided would, like the Appendices, have suffered very little if they had been published separately. Book I., entitled *Some Origins of Present Problems of Industry and Trade*, is a history of the claims to industrial leadership of

England, France, Germany, and the United States, mainly during the second half of the nineteenth century. Book II., on *Dominant Tendencies of Business Organisation,* whilst not definitely historical, is also in the main an account of the evolution of the forms of Business Organisation during the second half of the nineteenth century. Book I. is an account of the economic evolution of that period considered nationally; Book II. is an account of it considered technically. Book III., on *Monopolistic Tendencies: their Relations to Public Well-being,* deals in more detail with the special problems which arose in regard to Transport and to Trusts, Cartels, and Combinations during the same period.

Thus such unity as the book possesses derives from its being an account of the forms of individualistic capitalism as this had established itself in Western Europe at about the year 1900, of how they came to pass, and of how far they served the public interest. The volume as a whole also serves to illustrate what Marshall was always concerned to emphasise, namely, the transitory and changing character of the forms of business organisation and of the shapes in which economic activities embody themselves. He calls particular attention to the precarious and impermanent nature of the foundations on which England's industrial leadership had been built up.

The chief value of the book lies, however, in something less definite and more diffused than its central themes. It represents the fruits of Marshall's learning and ripe wisdom on a host of different matters. The book is a mine rather than a railway—like the *Principles*, a thing to quarry in and search for buried treasure. Like the *Principles*, again, it appears to be an easy book; yet it is more likely, I believe, to be useful to one who knows something already than to a beginner. It contains the suggestions, the starting points for many investigations. There is no better book for suggesting lines of original inquiry to a reader so disposed. But for the ignorant the broad generalisations of the book are too quiet, smooth, urbane, undogmatic, to catch him.

Industry and Trade was a remarkable success with the public. A second edition was called for immediately, and by the end of 1932, 16,000 copies had been printed. The fact that it was reaching wide circles of readers and met with no damaging criticisms was a cause of great encouragement and consolation to the aged author, who could feel that, after all, he had not been prevented by time, the enemy, from delivering his words to the world.

ALFRED MARSHALL

1920

But, all the same, time's wingèd chariot was hurrying near. "Old age," as he wrote in the preface to *Industry and Trade*, "indicates that my time for thought and speech is nearly ended." The composition of great Treatises is not, like that of great pictures, a work which can be continued into extreme old age. Much of his complete scheme of ordered knowledge would never be delivered. Yet his determination and his courage proved just equal to the publication of one more volume.

His powers of concentration and of memory were now beginning to fail somewhat rapidly. More and more he had to live for the book alone and to save for that every scrap of his strength. Talk with visitors tired him too much and interfered too seriously with his power of work. More and more Mrs. Marshall had to keep them away from him, and he lived alone with her, struggling with Time. He would rest much, listening to his favourite melodies on the auto-piano, which was a great solace to him during the last ten years of his life, or hearing Mrs. Marshall read over again a familiar novel. Each night he walked alone in the dark along the Madingley Road. On his seventy-eighth birthday he said that he did not much want a future life. When Mrs. Marshall asked him whether he would not like to return to this world at intervals of (say) a hundred years, to see what was happening, he replied that he should like it from pure curiosity. "My own thoughts," he went on, "turn more and more on the millions of worlds which may have reached a high state of morality before ours became habitable, and the other millions of worlds that may have a similar development after our sun has become cool and our world uninhabitable." [1] His greatest difficulty, he said, about believing in a future life was that he did not know at what stage of existence it could begin. One could hardly believe that apes had a future life or even the early stages of tree-dwelling human beings. Then at what stage could such an immense change as a future life begin?

Weaknesses of digestion, which had troubled him all his life, increased in later years. In September 1921, in his eightieth year, he made the following notes:

Tendency of work to bring on feeling of pressure in the head, accompanied by weariness, is increasing; and it troubles me. I must work on, so far as strength permits, for about two full years (or say four years of half-time) if that is allowed to me: after that, I can say "Nunc dimittis." I care little for length of life for

---

[1] Cf. the remarkable footnote to p. 101 of *Money, Credit and Commerce*.

its own sake. I want only so to arrange my work as to increase my chance of saying those things which I think of chief importance.

In August 1922, soon after his eightieth birthday, *Money, Credit and Commerce* was finished, and it was published in the following year, 1923.[1] The scope of the volume differed from his design, in that it did not include "a study of the influences on the conditions of man's life and work which are exerted by the resources available for employment." But he managed to bring within the covers of a book his chief contributions to the theories of Money and of Foreign Trade. The book is mainly pieced together from earlier fragments, some of them written fifty years before, as has been recorded above, where also the nature of his main contributions to these subjects have been summarised. It shows the marks of old age in a way which *Industry and Trade* did not. But it contains a quantity of materials and ideas, and collects together passages which are otherwise inaccessible to the student or difficult of access. "If much of it might have been written in the eighties of last century," Professor Edgeworth wrote of it in the *Economic Journal*, "much of it will be read in the eighties of this century."

[1] 5000 copies were sold immediately, and 9000 had been printed altogether by the end of 1932.

"Although old age presses on me," he wrote in the preface to *Money, Credit and Commerce*, "I am not without hopes that some of the notions which I have formed as to the possibilities of social advance may yet be published." Up to his last illness, in spite of loss of memory and great feebleness of body, he struggled to piece together one more volume. It was to have been called *Progress: its Economic Conditions*. But the task was too great. In a way his faculties were still strong. In writing a short letter he was still himself. One day in his eighty-second year he said that he was going to look at Plato's *Republic*, for he would like to try and write about the kind of Republic that Plato would wish for had he lived now. But though, as of old, he would sit and write, no advance was possible.

In these last days, with deep-set and shining eyes, wisps of white hair, and black cap on his head, he bore, more than ever, the aspect of a Sage or Prophet. At length his strength ebbed from him. But he would wake each morning, forgetful of his condition and thinking to begin his day's work as usual. On July 13, 1924, a fortnight before his eighty-second birthday, he passed away into rest.

[*Photo. Russell & Sons*

F. Y. EDGEWORTH

FRANCIS YSIDRO EDGEWORTH
1845–1926

FRANCIS YSIDRO EDGEWORTH was almost the last in the male line of a famous family—illustrating his own favourite Law of Averages; for his great-great-grandfather, Francis Edgeworth, married three wives,[1] and his grandfather, the eccentric and celebrated Richard Lovell Edgeworth, married four wives[2] and had twenty-two children, of whom seven sons and eight daughters survived him. F. Y. Edgeworth himself was the fifth son of a sixth son. Yet, in 1911, after the other heirs had died without leaving male issue,[3] he succeeded to the family estate of

[1] *Memoirs of Richard Lovell Edgeworth*, vol. i. p. 15, where many entertaining stories may be found of Edgeworth's forbears. This Francis has to-day no representatives in the male line in the Old World.

[2] His last wife, F. Y. Edgeworth's grandmother, under whose roof at Edgeworthstown he lived for the first twenty years of his life, survived until 1865, a hundred and twenty-one years after her husband's birth and her own ninety-sixth year.

[3] The eldest son of Richard Lovell, after being educated on Rousseau principles in early youth, emigrated to America and predeceased his father, who cut his American grandsons out of the estates. I am told that there are Edgeworths in the United States to-day who claim descent from this son.

Edgeworthstown, Co. Longford, where the Edgeworths, whose name was taken from Edgeware, formerly Edgeworth, in Middlesex, had established themselves in the reign of Queen Elizabeth. After his succession he had taken interest in gathering up family records and in seeking to restore Edgeworthstown House to something of its former tradition under the care of a married niece, Mrs. Montagu. Whilst visiting Ireland every summer, he did not live at Edgeworthstown, but declared that he looked forward to a happy "old age"—though when, if ever, he would have deemed this period to have arrived I do not know [1]—in the home of his forefathers.

Edgeworth was a notable link with celebrities of almost a century ago—a nephew of the novelist Maria Edgeworth,[2] who was born in 1767 and was already famous in the eighteenth

[1] He was ashamed, and not proud, of his years, and enjoined on me most seriously to make no reference in the *Economic Journal*, as I had desired to do, to his eightieth birthday, on the ground that he did not like to be connected with suggestions of senility and incapacity. His was:

> An age that melts in unperceiv'd decay
> And glides in modest innocence away.

[2] Edgeworth's father Frank was, in fact, the hero of several of Maria's tales. But (according to T. Mozley, *Reminiscences*, vol. i. p. 41) "Maria Edgeworth cared for the actual Frank as much as he cared for her, which was so little that it was better not to mention her." F. Y. E. remembered his Aunt Maria as "a very plain old lady with a delightful face" (*Black Book of Edgeworthstown*, p. 244). He was four years old when she died.

century, and a first cousin of the poet Thomas Lovell Beddoes, who died in 1847. Sir Walter Scott sent a copy of *Waverley* to Edgeworth's aunt on its first publication, and wrote in the last chapter of it (and afterwards in the preface to the novels) that it was her descriptions of Irish character which first encouraged him to make a similar experiment in Scotland; and Jane Austen sent her a copy of *Emma* on its first publication; and Macaulay sent her his *History*, which contains a reference to her. And in her later days she had visited Ricardo at Gatcomb Park.

F. Y. Edgeworth's father, Francis Beaufort Edgeworth, born in 1809, who had been educated at Charterhouse [1] and Cambridge, where he was a prominent member of Sterling's set, has been immortalised in none too flattering terms by Thomas Carlyle, who devoted some three pages to him in his *Life of John Sterling* (Part II. chap. iv.). "Frank was a short neat man," Carlyle wrote, "of sleek, square, colourless face (resembling the portraits of his Father),

[1] T. Mozley's account of him (*Reminiscences*, p. 41) is as follows: "He was a little fair-haired, blue-eyed, pale-faced fellow, ready and smooth of utterance, always with something in his head and on his tongue, and very much loved in a small circle at Charterhouse. With a fertile imagination and with infinite good-nature he would fall in with any idea for the time and help you on with it. . . . At school he was on Perpetual Motion, so often the first round in the ladder that leads nowhere."

with small blue eyes in which twinkled curiously a joyless smile; his voice was croaky and shrill, with a tone of shrewish obstinacy in it, and perhaps of sarcasm withal. A composed, dogmatic, speculative, exact, and not melodious man. He was learned in Plato and likewise in Kant; well-read in philosophies and literatures; entertained not creeds, but the Platonic or Kantian *ghosts* of creeds; coldly sneering away from him, in the joyless twinkle of those eyes, in the inexorable jingle of that shrill voice, all manner of Toryisms, superstitions: for the rest, a man of perfect veracity, of great diligence and other worth."

The Reverend Thomas Mozley, who devotes a chapter to Frank Edgeworth in his *Reminiscences*, does not confirm this account of "the good little Frank," as Carlyle calls him: "My ear still testifies that there was sweetness in Edgeworth's voice, and gentleness in his manner and tone. . . . Frank Edgeworth was torn by conflicting systems, and I may add conflicting sensibilities, from childhood. He was a most sympathetic, self - sacrificing being." [1] In Sterling's own description one can gain a further glimpse of the inherited temperament of the son. "Edgeworth seems to me not to have yet gone beyond a mere notional life. It

[1] *Reminiscences*, vol. i. p. 52.

is manifest that he has no knowledge of the necessity of a progress from *Wissen* to *Wesen* (say, *Knowing* to *Being*). . . . I regard it as a very happy thing for Edgeworth that he has come to England. In Italy he probably would never have gained any intuition into the reality of Being as different from a mere power of Speculating and Perceiving; and, of course, without this he can never reach to more than the merest Gnosis; which taken alone is a poor inheritance, a box of title-deeds to an estate which is covered with lava, or sunk under the sea." [1]

But Sterling's friend was only one of the ingredients which went to the making of Francis Ysidro Edgeworth. For Francis Beaufort Edgeworth "had married a young Spanish wife, whom by a romantic accident he came upon in London." [2] Edgeworth's mother was a Spanish lady, Rosa Florentina Eroles. Frank Edgeworth, on his way to Germany to study philosophy in the company of his nephew, T. L. Beddoes, stopped in London to read in the British Museum, and accidentally made the acquaintance of Senorita Eroles, aged sixteen, daughter of a political refugee from Catalonia, married her within three weeks, and carried her off to Florence, where the couple lived for a few

---

[1] Hare's *Sterling*, p. lxxiv.   [2] Carlyle, *loc. cit.*

years. F. Y. Edgeworth was a good linguist,
reading French, German, Spanish, and Italian,
and his mixed Irish-Spanish-French [1] origin
may have contributed to the markedly international sympathies of his mind.

The external landmarks of Edgeworth's life
are soon told. He was born at Edgeworthstown House, where, after returning from
Florence and an unsuccessful attempt at school-
mastering, Frank Edgeworth had settled down
to manage the family property, on February 8,
1845. His father died when he was two years
old. He was brought up at Edgeworthstown
under tutors until he went to Trinity College,
Dublin, at the age of seventeen. His memory
and agility of mind were already at that time
remarkable. He told his Oxford cousins [2] only
a few weeks before his death how well he still
remembered the poetry he had learnt in his
youth, and complete books of Milton, Pope,
Virgil, and Homer would readily come to his
memory. At the end of his life he was one of
the very few survivors of the tradition of free

[1] His great-grandfather was Daniel Augustus Beaufort, the
son of a French Huguenot refugee. A genealogical record of the
Beaufort family and of the Edgeworths connected with them will
be found in *The Family of the Beaufort in France, Holland, Germany,
and England*, by W. M. Beaufort, printed for private circulation in
1886.

[2] Mrs. A. G. Butler and her daughter, Miss C. V. Butler, to
whom I am much indebted for some of the foregoing particulars.

quotation from the Classics on all occasions and in all contexts.[1]

He entered Oxford as a scholar of Magdalen Hall, proceeding from there to Balliol, where he obtained a First Class in *Lit. Hum.* There is a tradition in Oxford concerning his "Viva" in the Final Schools. It is said that, being asked some abstruse question, he inquired, "Shall I answer briefly, or at length?" and then spoke for half an hour in a manner which converted what was to have been a Second Class into a First. He was called to the Bar by the Inner Temple in 1877, and spent some years in London with but straitened means, the youngest son of a younger son of an impoverished Irish estate, before he could find, amidst the multiplicity of his intellectual gifts and interests, his final direction. He became a Lecturer in Logic and afterwards Tooke Professor of Political Economy at King's College, London. In 1891 he succeeded Thorold Rogers as Drummond Professor of Political Economy at Oxford, and was elected a Fellow of All Souls, which became his home for the rest of his life. He retired from the Oxford professorship with the title of Emeritus Professor in 1922. He was President of the Economic Section of the British Association in 1889 and again in 1922.

[1] Like his grandfather before him, as Maria Edgeworth records.

T

He was an ex-President of the Royal Statistical Society, a Vice-President of the Royal Economic Society, and a Fellow of the British Academy. Above all, Edgeworth was the first Editor of the *Economic Journal* and designed and moulded it. He had been continuously responsible for it as Editor, Chairman of the Editorial Board, and Joint Editor from the first issue in March 1891 down to the day of his death, February 13, 1926. As his fellow-editor I received a final letter from him about its business after the news of his death.

At Balliol, Edgeworth had been a favourite of Jowett's, and it may have been from Jowett, who was always much interested in Political Economy and was occasionally teaching the subject at about that time, that he received his first impulse to the subject. The most important influence, however, on his early economic thought was, I think, Jevons, whom he got to know in London, where his Hampstead lodgings were but a short distance from Jevons' house. His contact with Marshall, for whom his respect was unmeasured, came a little later. In *The Academy* for 1881, Marshall reviewed Edgeworth's *Mathematical Psychics*—one of the two only reviews which Marshall ever wrote, the other being of Jevons' *Theory of Political Economy*. This review led to an acquaintanceship which ripened into a lifelong personal and intellectual friendship. Mrs. Marshall has many pleasant memories of Edgeworth's visits to Cambridge—though there can seldom have been a couple whose conversational methods were less suited to one another than Francis Edgeworth and Alfred Marshall.

To judge from his published works, Edgeworth reached Economics, as Marshall had before him, through Mathematics and Ethics. But here the resemblance ceases. Marshall's interest was intellectual and moral, Edgeworth's intellectual and aesthetic. Edgeworth wished to establish *theorems* of intellectual and aesthetic interest, Marshall to establish *maxims* of practical and moral importance. In respect of technical training and of lightness and security of touch, Marshall was much his superior in the mathematical field—Marshall had been Second Wrangler, Edgeworth had graduated in *Litteris Humanioribus*. Yet Edgeworth, clumsy and awkward though he often was in his handling of the mathematical instrument, was in originality, in accomplishment, and in the bias of his natural interest considerably the greater mathematician. I do not think it can be disputed that for forty years Edgeworth was the most distinguished and the most prolific exponent in the world of what he himself dubbed

Mathematical Psychics—the niceties and the broadnesses of the application of quasi-mathematical method to the Social Sciences.

It would be a formidable task to draw up a complete list of Edgeworth's writings,[1] almost entirely in the shape of contributions to learned journals. The earliest with which I am acquainted is his *New and Old Methods of Ethics*, published by Parker and Co. of Oxford in 1877, when he was thirty-two years of age—a paper-covered volume of 92 pages. It mainly consists of a discussion of the quantitative problems which arise in an examination of Utilitarianism, in the form of a commentary on Sidgwick's *Methods of Ethics* and Barratt's criticisms of Sidgwick in *Mind* for 1877. Edgeworth's peculiarities of style, his brilliance of phrasing, his obscurity of connection, his inconclusiveness of aim, his restlessness of direction, his courtesy, his caution, his shrewdness, his wit, his subtlety, his learning, his reserve—all are

[1] A list of twenty-five books and papers, published between 1877 and 1887, is to be found in an Appendix to his *Metretike*. I have recorded twenty-nine items, which bear on the Theory of Probability, ranging between 1883 and 1921 and partly overlapping with the above, in the bibliographical appendix to my *Treatise on Probability*. Thirty-four papers on Economics and seventy-five reviews are reprinted in his *Papers relating to Political Economy*. The Royal Statistical Society has published a Memoir by Prof. A. L. Bowley on *Edgeworth's Contributions to Mathematical Statistics* at the end of which there is an annotated bibliography covering seventy-four papers and nine reviews.

there full-grown. Quotations from the Greek tread on the heels of the differential calculus, and the philistine reader can scarcely tell whether it is a line of Homer or a mathematical abstraction which is in course of integration. The concluding words of Edgeworth's first flight would have come as well at the end of his long travelling:

Where the great body of moral science is already gone before, from all sides ascending, under a master's guidance, towards one serene commanding height, thither aspires this argument, a straggler coming up, *non passibus aequis*, and by a devious route. A devious route, and verging to the untrodden method which was fancifully delineated in the previous section; so far at least as the mathematical handling of pleasures is divined to be conducive to a genuinely physical ethic, προοίμια αὐτοῦ τοῦ νόμου.

Another slim volume (150 pages), *Mathematical Psychics: An Essay on the Application of Mathematics to the Moral Sciences*, appeared in 1881. This was Edgeworth's first contribution to Economics and contains some of the best work he ever did.[1] During the last months of his life he nursed the intention of reprinting a portion of it.[2]

[1] A paper entitled "Hedonical Calculus," which is reprinted in *Mathematical Psychics*, had appeared meanwhile in *Mind*, 1879.

[2] In 1932 a facsimile reprint of this book was issued in the London School of Economics Series of *Reprints of Scarce Tracts*.

The volume on Ethics had attempted to apply mathematical method to Utilitarianism. In *Mathematical Psychics* Edgeworth carried his treatment of "the calculus of *Feeling*, of Pleasure and Pain" a stage further. The Essay consists of two parts "concerned respectively with principle and practice, root and fruit, the applicability and the application of Mathematics to Sociology." In the First Part, which is very short, "it is attempted to illustrate the possibility of Mathematical reasoning without *numerical* data"—a thesis which at the time it was written was of much originality and importance. "We cannot *count* the golden sands of life; we cannot *number* the 'innumerable' smiles of seas of love; but we seem to be capable of observing that there is here a *greater*, there a *less*, multitude of pleasure-units, mass of happiness; and that is enough."

The Second Part contains the roots of much of Edgeworth's work on mathematical economics, in particular the treatment of Contract in a free market and its possible indeterminateness; and it is here that his famous *Contract-Curves* first appear.

I have dwelt on these two early works at disproportionate length, because in them, and particularly in *Mathematical Psychics*, the full flavour and peculiarity of Edgeworth's mind and art are exhibited without reserve. The latter is a very eccentric book and open to mockery. In later works, it seems to me, Edgeworth did not ever give quite a full rein to his natural self. He feared a little the philistine comment on the strange but charming amalgam of poetry and pedantry, science and art, wit and learning, of which he had the secret; and he would endeavour, however unsuccessfully, to draw a veil of partial concealment over his native style, which only served, however, to enhance the obscurity and allusiveness and half-apologetic air with which he served up his intellectual dishes. The problem of the inequality of men's and women's wages interested him all his life and was the subject of his Presidential address to Section F of the British Association in 1922; but who in space and time but Edgeworth in the eighties, whose sly chuckles one can almost hear as one reads, would treat it thus:

The aristocracy of sex is similarly grounded upon the supposed superior capacity of the man for happiness, for the ἐνεργεῖαι of action and contemplation; upon the sentiment:

Woman is the lesser man, and her passions unto mine
Are as moonlight unto sunlight and as water unto wine.

Her supposed generally inferior capacity is supposed to be compensated by a special capacity for particular

emotions, certain kinds of beauty and refinement.
Agreeably to such finer sense of beauty, the modern
lady has received a larger share of certain *means*, certain
luxuries and attentions (Def. 2; *a sub finem*). But
gallantry, that "mixed sentiment which took its rise in
the ancient chivalry," has many other elements. It is
explained by the polite Hume as attention to the weak,
and by the passionate Rousseau $\phi \upsilon \sigma \iota \kappa \omega \tau \acute{\epsilon} \rho \omega s$ . . . .
Altogether, account being taken of existing, whether
true or false, opinions about the nature of woman,
there appears a nice consilience between the deductions
from the utilitarian principle and the disabilities and
privileges which hedge round modern womanhood.[1]

Edgeworth next proceeded to the second
great application of mathematics to the Moral
Sciences, namely, its application "to *Belief*, the
Calculus of Probabilities," which became perhaps his favourite study of all. In 1883 and
1884 he contributed seven papers on Probability and the Law of Error to the *Philosophical
Magazine*, to *Mind*, and to *Hermathena*. These
were the first of a very long series of which the
last, one more elaborate discussion of the
Generalised Law of Error, still remained at
the date of his death to appear in the *Statistical
Journal*.

As regards Probability proper, Edgeworth's
most important writings are his article on "The
Philosophy of Chance" in *Mind*, 1884, and on

[1] *Mathematical Psychics*, p. 78.

"Probability" in the *Encyclopaedia Britannica*
(revised up to 1911). Edgeworth began as an
adherent of the Frequency Theory of Probability, with a strong bias in favour of a physical
rather than a logical basis for the conception,
just as he was an adherent of the Utilitarian
Ethics with a bias in favour of a physical rather
than a metaphysical basis. But in both cases
his mind was alive to the objections, and in both
cases the weight of the objections increased in
his mind, as time went on, rather than diminished. Nevertheless, he did not in either case
replace these initial presumptions by any others,
with the result that he took up increasingly a
sceptical attitude towards philosophical foundations combined with a pragmatic attitude towards practical applications which had been
successfully erected upon them, however in-
secure these foundations might really be. The
consequence was that the centre of his interest
gradually passed from Probability to the Theory
of Statistics, and from Utilitarianism to the
Marginal Theory of Economics. I have often
pressed him to give an opinion as to how far the
modern theory of Statistics and Correlation can
stand if the Frequency Theory falls as a logical
doctrine. He would always reply to the effect
that the collapse of the Frequency Theory would
affect the *universality* of application of Statistical

Theory, but that large masses of statistical data did, nevertheless, in his opinion, satisfy the conditions required for the validity of Statistical Theory, whatever these might be. I expect that this is true. It is a reasonable attitude for one who is mainly interested in statistics to take up. But it implied in Edgeworth an unwillingness to revise or take up again the more speculative studies of his youth. The same thing was true of his work in Economics. He was disinclined, in company with most other economists of the Classical School, to reconsider how far the initial assumptions of the Marginal Theory stand or fall with the Utilitarian Ethics and the Utilitarian Psychology, out of which they sprang and which were sincerely accepted, in a way no one accepts them now, by the founders of the subject. Mill, Jevons, the Marshall of the seventies, and the Edgeworth[1] of the late seventies and the early eighties *believed* the Utilitarian Psychology and laid the foundations of the subject in this belief. The later Marshall and the later Edgeworth and many of the younger generation have not fully believed; but we still trust the superstructure

[1] In his early adherence to Utilitarianism Edgeworth reacted back again from his father's reaction against Maria Edgeworth's philosophy in these matters. Mozley (*op. cit.*) records of Frank Edgeworth that "he showed an early and strong revolt against the hollowness, callousness, and deadness of utilitarianism."

without exploring too thoroughly the soundness of the original foundations.

Thus, as time went on, Edgeworth's technical statistical work became more important than his contributions to the theory of probability. From 1885 onwards his more general articles, especially his "Methods of Statistics" in the Jubilee Volume of the *Statistical Journal*, 1885, and his "Application of the Calculus of Probabilities to Statistics" in the *Bulletin of the International Statistical Institute*, 1910, were of great value in keeping English students in touch with the work of the German school founded by Lexis and in sponsoring, criticising, and applauding from their first beginnings the work of the English statisticians on Correlation. His constructive work, particularly in his later years, centred in highly elaborate and difficult discussions of his own "Generalised Law of Error." Edgeworth's particular affection for the mode of treatment which he here adopted was partly due, I think, to its requiring the minimum of assumption, so that he was able to obtain his results on more generalised hypotheses than will yield results in the case of other statistical formulae. In this way he could compensate, as it were, his bad conscience about the logical, as distinct from the pragmatic, grounds of current statistical theory.

At about the same time as his first papers on Probability and the Law of Error, namely, in 1883, in his thirty-eighth year, Edgeworth embarked on the fifth topic, which was to complete the range of the main work of his life, that is to say, Index Numbers, or the application of mathematical method to the measurement of economic value.[1] These five applications of Mathematical Psychics—to the measurement of Utility or ethical value, to the algebraic or diagrammatic determination of economic equilibriums, to the measurement of Belief or Probability, to the measurement of Evidence or Statistics, and to the measurement of economic value or Index Numbers—constitute, with their extensions and ramifications and illustrations, Edgeworth's life work. If he had been of the kind that produce Treatises, he would doubtless have published, some time between 1900 and 1914, a large volume in five books entitled *Mathematical Psychics*. But this was not to be. He followed up his two monographs of 1877 and 1881 with a third entitled *Metretike, or the Method of Measuring Probability and Utility*, in 1887. It is a

---

[1] I refer to Edgeworth's first contribution to the *Statistical Journal* (1883), "The Method of ascertaining a Change in the Value of Gold." This was followed by the well-known memoranda presented to the British Association in 1887, 1888, and 1889, and a long series of articles thereafter, several of which are reprinted in his *Collected Papers*, vol. i.

disappointing volume and not much worth reading (a judgement with which I know that Edgeworth himself concurred). After this, so far from rising from the Monograph to the Treatise, moving to the opposite extreme from Marshall's, he sank from the Monograph to the paper, essay, article, or transaction. For forty years a long stream of splinters split off from his bright mind to illumine (and to obscure) the pages of the *Statistical* and *Economic Journals*.

Once when I asked him why he had never ventured on a Treatise he answered, with his characteristic smile and chuckle, that large-scale enterprise, such as Treatises and marriage, had never appealed to him. It may be that he deemed them industries subject to diminishing return, or that they lay outside his powers or the limits he set to his local universe. Such explanations are more than enough and Occam's razor should forbid me to mention another. But there may have been a contributory motive.

Mathematical Psychics has not, as a science or study, fulfilled its early promise. In the seventies and eighties of the last century it was reasonable, I think, to suppose that it held great prospects. When the young Edgeworth chose it, he may have looked to find secrets as wonderful as those which the physicists have found since those days. But, as I remarked in writing about Alfred Marshall's gradual change of attitude towards mathematico-economics (p. 192 above), this has not happened, but quite the opposite. The atomic hypothesis which has worked so splendidly in Physics breaks down in Psychics. We are faced at every turn with the problems of Organic Unity, of Discreteness, of Discontinuity—the whole is not equal to the sum of the parts, comparisons of quantity fail us, small changes produce large effects, the assumptions of a uniform and homogeneous continuum are not satisfied. Thus the results of Mathematical Psychics turn out to be derivative, not fundamental, indexes, not measurements, first approximations at the best; and fallible indexes, dubious approximations at that, with much doubt added as to what, if anything, they are indexes or approximations of. No one was more conscious of all this than Edgeworth. All his intellectual life through he felt his foundations slipping away from under him. What wonder that with these hesitations added to his cautious, critical, sceptical, diffident nature the erection of a large and heavy superstructure did not appeal to him. Edgeworth knew that he was skating on thin ice; and as life went on his love of skating and his distrust of the ice increased, by a malicious fate, *pari passu*. He is like one who seeks to avert the evil eye by looking sideways, to escape the censure of fate by euphemism, calling the treacherous sea Euxine and the unfriendly guardians of Truth the kindly ones. Edgeworth seldom looked the reader or interlocutor straight in the face; he is allusive, obscure, and devious as one who would slip by unnoticed, hurrying on if stopped by another traveller.

After the appearance of *Metretike* in 1887, Edgeworth ventured on no separate publication, apart from four lectures delivered during the war, which were printed in pamphlet form,[1] until in 1925 the Royal Economic Society published under his own editorship his *Collected Economic Papers* in three substantial volumes. These volumes preserve in accessible form the whole of Edgeworth's contributions to the subject of Economics, which he himself wished to see preserved, apart from some portions of *Mathematical Psychics* alluded to above.

The publication of his Economic Papers was a great satisfaction to Edgeworth. His modest and self-effacing ways would always have prevented him from undertaking such an enterprise on his own initiative. But as soon as

---

[1] *On the Relations of Political Economy to War, The Cost of War, Currency and Finance in Time of War,* and *A Levy on Capital.* None of these is amongst his best work.

others were prepared to take the responsibility, the business of selection and preparation for the press was a congenial task. Moreover, the publication proved a great success in every way, and was reviewed in learned journals throughout the world with expressions of esteem such as the author's previous modes of publication had cut him off from hearing. I think that Edgeworth was genuinely surprised at the extent of his international reputation, and it gave him as much pleasure as surprise.

In spite of his constant flow of learned papers, a great part of Edgeworth's time for the last thirty-five years of his life was occupied with the editorship of the *Economic Journal*. His practical gifts as an editor were quite other than might have been expected from his reputation as an unpractical, unbusinesslike person, remote from affairs, living on abstractions in the clouds, illuminating the obscure by the more obscure. As one who was associated with him in the conduct of the *Journal* for fifteen years, I can report that this picture was the opposite of the truth. He was punctual, businesslike, and dependable in the conduct of all routine matters. He was quite incapable of detecting misprints in what he wrote himself,[1] but had an excep-

[1] The difficulty of his articles was often enhanced by the fact that they were packed with misprints, especially in the symbolic parts.

tionally sharp eye for other people's.   He had
an unfailing instinct for good "copy" (except,
again, in what he wrote himself), exercised his
editorial powers with great strictness to secure
brevity from the contributors,[1] and invariably
cast his influence in favour of matter having
topical interest and against tedious expositions
of methodology and the like (which often, in his
opinion, rendered German journals unuseful).
I have often found myself in the position of
defending the heavier articles against his
strictures.   He established and was always
anxious to maintain the international sympathies
and affiliations of the *Journal*.   I am sure that
there was no economist in England better read
than he in foreign literature.   He added to this
what must have been the widest personal acquaintance in the world with economists of all
nations.   Edgeworth was the most hospitable
of men, and there can have been very few foreign
economists, whether of established reputation
or not, who visited London in his time and were
not entertained by Edgeworth.   He had a
strong feeling for the solidarity of economic
science throughout the world and sought to
encourage talent wherever he found it, and to

---

[1] He invented and attached much importance to what he
termed a law of diminishing returns in the remuneration of
articles, by which the rate falls after ten pages have been exceeded
and sinks to zero after twenty pages.

U

extend courtesies in the most exquisite traditions of Ireland and Spain. His tolerance was all-embracing, and he combined a respect for established reputation which might have been thought excessive if there had not been a flavour of mockery in it, with a natural inclination to encourage the youthful and the unknown. All his eccentricity and artistic strangeness found its outlet in his own writings. All his practical good sense and daily shrewdness was devoted to the *Economic Journal*.

On anyone who knew Edgeworth he must have made a strong individual impression as a person. But it is scarcely possible to portray him to those who did not. He was kind, affectionate, modest, self-depreciatory, humorous, with a sharp and candid eye for human nature; he was also reserved, angular, complicated, proud, and touchy, elaborately polite, courteous to the point of artificiality, absolutely unbending and unyielding in himself to the pressure of the outside world. Marshall, remembering his mixed parentage, used to say: "Francis is a charming fellow, but you must be careful with Ysidro."

His health and vigour of body were exceptional. He was still a climber in the mountains, bather in the cold waters of the morning at Parson's Pleasure, unwearying pedestrian in the meadows of Oxfordshire, after he had passed his seventieth year.   He was always at work, reading, correcting proofs, "verifying references" (a vain pursuit upon which his ostensible reverence for authority and disinclination to say anything definite on his own responsibility led him to waste an abundance of time), working out on odd bits of paper long arithmetical examples of abstruse theorems which he loved to do (just as Maria Edgeworth has recorded of his grandfather), writing letters, building up his lofty constructions with beautiful bricks but too little mortar and no clear architectural design. Towards the end of his life it was not easy to carry through with him a consecutive argument *viva voce*—he had a certain dissatisfied restlessness of body and attention which increased with age and was not good to see.   But on paper his intellectual powers even after his eightieth year were entirely unabated; and he died, as he would have wished, in harness.

Edgeworth was never married; but it was not for want of susceptibility. His difficult nature, not his conception of life, cut him off from a full intimacy in any direction. He did not have as much happiness as he might have had. But in many ways a bachelor life suited his character. He liked to have the fewest possible material cares; he did not want to be

loaded with any sort of domestic responsibility;
and he was content without private comfort.
No one lived more continuously than he in
Common Rooms, Libraries, and Clubs, or depended more completely upon such adjuncts for
every amenity. He had but few possessions—
scarcely any furniture or crockery, not even
books (he preferred a public library near at hand),
no proper notepaper of his own or stationery or
stamps. Red tape and gum are the only material
objects with the private ownership of which I
associate him. But he was particular about his
appearance, and was well dressed in his own
style. There was more of Spain than of Edgeworth in his looks. With broad forehead, long
nose, olive colouring, trimly pointed beard, and
strong hands, his aspect was distinguished but
a little belied by his air of dwelling *uncomfortably*
in his clothes or in his body. He lived at
Oxford in spartanic rooms at All Souls; in
London lodgings at 5 Mount Vernon, two small
bare rooms, pitched high on the cliff of Hampstead with a wide view over the metropolitan
plain, which he had taken on a weekly tenancy
more than fifty years before and had occupied ever
since; in Ireland, where he would spend some
weeks of the summer, at the St. George Club,
Kingstown. For meals the Buttery and Hall of
All Souls, the Athenaeum, the Savile, or the

Albemarle; for books the libraries of these places, of the British Museum, of Trinity College, Dublin, of the Royal Statistical Society.

It is narrated that in his boyhood at Edgeworthstown he would read Homer seated aloft in a heron's nest. So, as it were, he dwelt always, not too much concerned with the earth.

F. P. RAMSEY

I. Ramsey as an Economist

The death at the age of twenty-six of Frank
Ramsey, Fellow of King's College, Cambridge,
sometime scholar of Winchester and of Trinity,
son of the President of Magdalene, was a heavy
loss—though his primary interests were in
Philosophy and Mathematical Logic—to the
pure theory of Economics. From a very early
age, about sixteen I think, his precocious mind
was intensely interested in economic problems.
Economists living in Cambridge have been
accustomed from his undergraduate days to try
their theories on the keen edge of his critical
and logical faculties. If he had followed the
easier path of mere inclination, I am not sure
that he would not have exchanged the tor-
menting exercises of the foundations of thought
and of psychology, where the mind tries to catch
its own tail, for the delightful paths of our own
most agreeable branch of the moral sciences, in
which theory and fact, intuitive imagination and

FRANK RAMSEY

Aged 18

practical judgement, are blended in a manner comfortable to the human intellect.

When he did descend from his accustomed stony heights, he still lived without effort in a rarer atmosphere than most economists care to breathe, and handled the technical apparatus of our science with the easy grace of one accustomed to something far more difficult. But he has left behind him in print (apart from his philosophical papers) only two witnesses to his powers—his papers published in the *Economic Journal* on "A Contribution to the Theory of Taxation" in March 1927, and on "A Mathematical Theory of Saving" in December 1928. The latter of these is, I think, one of the most remarkable contributions to mathematical economics ever made, both in respect of the intrinsic importance and difficulty of its subject, the power and elegance of the technical methods employed, and the clear purity of illumination with which the writer's mind is felt by the reader to play about its subject. The article is terribly difficult reading for an economist, but it is not difficult to appreciate how scientific and aesthetic qualities are combined in it together.

The loss of Ramsey is, therefore, to his friends, for whom his personal qualities joined most harmoniously with his intellectual powers, one which it will take them long to forget. His

bulky Johnsonian frame, his spontaneous gurg-
ling laugh, the simplicity of his feelings and
reactions, half-alarming sometimes and occasionally almost cruel in their directness and
literalness, his honesty of mind and heart, his
modesty, and the amazing, easy efficiency of
the intellectual machine which ground away
behind his wide temples and broad, smiling face,
have been taken from us at the height of their
excellence and before their harvest of work and
life could be gathered in.

March 1930.

II. RAMSEY AS A PHILOSOPHER

Logic, like lyrical poetry, is no employment
for the middle-aged, and it may be that we have
in this volume [1] some of the best illumination
which one of the brightest minds of our generation could give, though he died at twenty-six.
I do not think that there is any book of equal
importance for those who would think about
fundamental matters in a modern way, and the
circumstance that much of it is tentative and
inconclusive and not finally corrected is no impediment in a subject where an author's vanity

[1] *The Foundations of Mathematics.* By F. P. Ramsey. Kegan
Paul. 15s.

in giving his finished work a rounded surface is pure deception.

Seeing all of Frank Ramsey's logical essays published together, we can perceive quite clearly the direction which his mind was taking. It is a remarkable example of how the young can take up the story at the point to which the previous generation had brought it a little out of breath, and then proceed forward without taking more than about a week thoroughly to digest everything which had been done up to date, and to understand with apparent ease stuff which to anyone even ten years older seemed hopelessly difficult. One almost has to believe that Ramsey in his nursery near Magdalene was unconsciously absorbing from 1903 to 1914 everything which anyone may have been saying or writing in Trinity. In the year 1903, in which Frank Ramsey was born, Bertrand Russell's *Principles of Mathematics* was published, giving a new life to formal logic and seeming to bring new kingdoms within its scope. This book raised certain fundamental problems without solving all of them satisfactorily, but for the next seven years Russell and Whitehead were more concentrated on the technical problem of exhibiting in their *Principia Mathematica* the actual links between mathematics and formal logic than on strengthening the foundations on which they were building. But meanwhile Ludwig Wittgenstein had been attracted to Cambridge by the desire to talk with Russell, and Wittgenstein was wholly occupied with the fundamental matters of logical analysis. His *Tractatus Logico-Philosophicus* was mainly worked out before the war, but it was not published until 1922, by which time Frank Ramsey was on the scene, aged nineteen, to assist in the preparation of an English version and to expound its obscure contents to the world. To-day, Russell is recognising that each period of life has its appropriate avocation, and that the fundamental exercises of logic are not for those who have reached their sixtieth year. Wittgenstein is wondering if his next book will be finished before time's chariots are too near, and Ramsey, alas! who entered into their harvest as easily as a young lord into his estates, is dead.

The first part of this book, comprising papers which have been previously published, consists in tackling fundamental problems at the point at which the work of Russell and Wittgenstein had left them. They are handled with great power, and at the same time elegance of treatment and lucidity, and probably with success. The second part, which has not previously been published, deals with Probability and associated subjects, starting from a criticism of my *Treatise on Probability*, which was published in 1921. This latter part had not been published because it was fragmentary and not completely satis-factory. But it is of the greatest interest both in itself and as showing in some detail how far his mind was departing, in pursuance of certain hints thrown out in the first part, from the formal and objective treatment of his immediate predecessors. The first impression conveyed by the work of Russell was that the field of formal logic was enormously extended. The gradual perfection of the formal treatment at the hands of himself, of Wittgenstein and of Ramsey had been, however, gradually to empty it of content and to reduce it more and more to mere dry bones, until finally it seemed to ex-clude not only all experience, but most of the principles, usually reckoned logical, of reason-able thought. Wittgenstein's solution was to regard everything else as a sort of inspired non-sense, having great value indeed for the indi-vidual, but incapable of being exactly discussed. Ramsey's reaction was towards what he himself described as a sort of pragmatism, not unsym-pathetic to Russell but repugnant to Wittgen-stein. "The essence of pragmatism," he says, "I take to be this, that the meaning of a sentence is to be defined by reference to the actions to which asserting it would lead, or, more vaguely still, by its possible causes and effects. Of this I feel certain, but of nothing more definite."

Thus he was led to consider "human logic" as distinguished from "formal logic." Formal logic is concerned with nothing but the rules of *consistent* thought. But in addition to this we have certain "useful mental habits" for handling the material with which we are supplied by our perceptions and by our memory and perhaps in other ways, and so arriving at or towards truth; and the analysis of such habits is also a sort of logic. The application of these ideas to the logic of probability is very fruitful. Ramsey argues, as against the view which I had put forward, that probability is concerned not with objective relations between propositions but (in some sense) with degrees of belief, and he succeeds in showing that the calculus of probabilities simply amounts to a set of rules for ensuring that the system of degrees of belief which we hold shall be a *consistent* system. Thus the calculus of probabilities belongs to formal logic. But the basis of our degrees of belief— or the *a priori* probabilities, as they used to be called—is part of our human outfit, perhaps given us merely by natural selection, analogous to our perceptions and our memories rather than to formal logic. So far I yield to Ramsey

—I think he is right. But in attempting to distinguish "rational" degrees of belief from belief in general he was not yet, I think, quite successful. It is not getting to the bottom of the principle of induction merely to say that it is a useful mental habit. Yet in attempting to distinguish a "human" logic from formal logic on the one hand and descriptive psychology on the other, Ramsey may have been pointing the way to the next field of study when formal logic has been put into good order and its highly limited scope properly defined.

Ramsey reminds one of Hume more than of anyone else, particularly in his common sense and a sort of hard-headed practicality towards the whole business. The reader will find many passages which convey the peculiar flavour of his mind, the expression of which—though not included by him amongst the purposes of philosophy!—was a delightful thing.

October 1931.

III. A Short Anthology

Most of Ramsey's writings, as published in the posthumous collection *The Foundations of Mathematics*, in the *Economic Journal,* and in the *Encyclopaedia Britannica,* are very technical.

But amongst his notes, not published in his lifetime and none of them polished for the press, which have been brought together at the end of *The Foundations of Mathematics* [1] are some aphorisms and fragmentary essays from which I give below a few selections, because they may convey a little of what I have called above "the peculiar flavour of his mind"; though nothing will ever fully convey to those, who never came into direct acquaintance with the workings of his intellect and personality as given to one in a single joint impression, why Mr. Braithwaite could write with justice that his death deprived Cambridge of one of its chief intellectual glories. Let me also quote what Goldsworthy Lowes Dickinson wrote of Frank Ramsey and of C. P. Sanger, another scholar of Winchester and Trinity, who died, though in his maturity, nearly at the same time:

It does not become a Cambridge man to claim too much for his university, nor am I much tempted to do so. But there is, I think, a certain type, rare, like all good things, which seems to be associated in some peculiar way with my alma mater. I am thinking of men like Leslie Stephen (the original of Meredith's Vernon Whitford), like Henry Sidgwick, like Maitland,

[1] Published by Messrs. Kegan Paul in 1931 under the editorship of Mr. R. B. Braithwaite. I am indebted to the publishers and the editor for permission to reproduce here the passages which follow.

FRANK RAMSEY

Aged 22

(Top of "Red Pike," June, 1925)

like one who died but the other day with all his promise
unfulfilled.   It is a type unworldly without being
saintly, unambitious without being inactive, warm-
hearted without being sentimental.   Through good
report and ill such men work on, following the light of
truth as they see it; able to be sceptical without being
paralyzed; content to know what is knowable and to
reserve judgment on what is not.   The world could
never be driven by such men, for the springs of action
lie deep in ignorance and madness.   But it is they who
are the beacon in the tempest, and they are more, not
less, needed now than ever before. May their succession
never fail!

---

1. *PHILOSOPHY*

PHILOSOPHY must be of some use and we must
take it seriously; it must clear our thoughts
and so our actions.   Or else it is a disposition
we have to check, and an inquiry to see that this
is so; *i.e.* the chief proposition of philosophy
is that philosophy is nonsense.   And again we
must then take seriously that it is nonsense,
and not pretend, as Wittgenstein does, that it is
important nonsense!

In philosophy we take the propositions we
make in science and everyday life and try to
exhibit them in a logical system with primitive
terms and definitions, etc.   Essentially a philosophy is a system of definitions or, only too

often, a system of descriptions of how definitions might be given.

I do not think it is necessary to say with Moore that the definitions explain what we have hitherto meant by our propositions, but rather that they show how we intend to use them in future. Moore would say they were the same, that philosophy does not change what anyone meant by "This is a table." It seems to me that it might; for meaning is mainly potential, and a change might therefore only be manifested on rare and critical occasions. Also, sometimes philosophy should clarify and distinguish notions previously vague and confused, and clearly this is meant to fix our future meaning only. But this is clear, that the definitions are to give at least our future meaning, and not merely to give any pretty way of obtaining a certain structure.

I used to worry myself about the nature of philosophy through excessive scholasticism. I could not see how we could understand a word and not be able to recognise whether a proposed definition of it was or was not correct. I did not realise the vagueness of the whole idea of understanding, the reference it involves to a multitude of performances any of which may fail and require to be restored. Logic issues in tautologies, mathematics in identities, philosophy in definitions; all trivial, but all part of the vital work of clarifying and organising our thought.[1]

2. PHILOSOPHICAL THINKING

It seems to me that in the process of clarifying our thought we come to terms and sentences which we cannot elucidate in the obvious manner by defining their meaning. For instance, theoretical terms we cannot define, but we can explain the way in which they are used, and in this explanation we are forced to look not only at the objects which we are talking about, but at our own mental states.

Now this means that we cannot get clear about these terms and sentences without getting clear about meaning, and we seem to get into the situation that we cannot understand, *e.g.* what we say about time and the external world without first understanding meaning, and yet we cannot understand meaning without first understanding certainly time and probably the external world which are involved in it. So we cannot make our philosophy into an ordered progress to a goal, but have to take our problems

[1] *The Foundations of Mathematics,* pp. 263, 264. In these quotations there are small omissions here and there which I have not in every case indicated. I hope readers will be led on to consult the full text of the original.

as a whole and jump to a simultaneous solution; which will have something of the nature of a hypothesis, for we shall accept it not as the consequence of direct argument, but as the only one we can think of which satisfies our several requirements.

Of course, we should not strictly speak of argument, but there is in philosophy a process analogous to "linear inference" in which things become successively clear; and since, for the above reason, we cannot carry this through to the end, we are in the ordinary position of scientists of having to be content with piecemeal improvements: we can make several things clearer, but we cannot make anything clear.

I find this self-consciousness inevitable in philosophy except in a very limited field. We are driven to philosophise because we do not know clearly what we mean; the question is always "What do I mean by x?" And only very occasionally can we settle this without reflecting on meaning. But it is not only an obstacle, this necessity of dealing with meaning; it is doubtless an essential clue to the truth. If we neglect it I feel we may get into the absurd position of the child in the following dialogue: "Say breakfast." "Can't." "What can't you say?" "Can't say breakfast."

The chief danger to our philosophy, apart

from laziness and woolliness, is scholasticism, the essence of which is treating what is vague as if it were precise and trying to fit it into an exact logical category. A typical piece of scholasticism is Wittgenstein's view that all our everyday propositions are completely in order and that it is impossible to think illogically. (This last is like saying that it is impossible to break the rules of bridge, because if you break them you are not playing bridge but, as Mrs. C. says, not-bridge.) [1]

3. *IS THERE ANYTHING TO DISCUSS?*

Science, history, and politics are not suited for discussion except by experts. Others are simply in the position of requiring more information, and, till they have acquired all available information, cannot do anything but accept on authority the opinions of those better qualified. Then there is philosophy; this, too, has become too technical for the layman. Besides this disadvantage, the conclusion of the greatest modern philosopher is that there is no such subject as philosophy; that it is an activity, not a doctrine; and that, instead of answering questions, it aims merely at curing headaches. It might be thought that, apart from this technical philosophy whose centre is logic, there

[1] *Op. cit.* pp. 267-69.

was a sort of popular philosophy which dealt
with such subjects as the relation of man to
nature, and the meaning of morality. But any
attempt to treat such topics seriously reduces
them to questions either of science or of technical
philosophy, or results more immediately in perceiving them to be nonsensical. . . .

I think we rarely, if ever, discuss fundamental psychological questions, but far more
often simply compare our several experiences,
which is not a form of discussing. I think we
realise too little how often our arguments are
of the form:—A: "I went to Grantchester this
afternoon." B: "No I didn't." Another thing
we often do is to discuss what sort of people or
behaviour we feel admiration for or ashamed of.
E.g. when we discuss constancy of affection it
consists in A saying he would feel guilty if he
weren't constant, B saying *he* wouldn't feel
guilty in the least. But that, although a pleasant
way of passing the time, is not discussing anything whatever, but simply comparing notes.

Genuine psychology, on the other hand, is a
science of which we most of us know far too
little for it to become us to venture an opinion.

Lastly, there is aesthetics, including literature. This always excites us far more than
anything else; but we don't really discuss it
much. Our arguments are so feeble; we are

still at the stage of "Who drives fat oxen must himself be fat," and have very little to say about the psychological problems of which aesthetics really consists, *e.g.* why certain combinations of colours give us such peculiar feelings. What we really like doing is again to compare our experience; a practice which in this case is peculiarly profitable because the critic can point out things to other people to which, if they attend, they will obtain feelings which they value which they failed to obtain otherwise. We do not and cannot discuss whether one work of art is better than another; we merely compare the feelings it gives.

I conclude that there really is nothing to discuss; and this conclusion corresponds to a feeling I have about ordinary conversation also. It is a relatively new phenomenon which has arisen from two causes which have operated gradually through the nineteenth century. One is the advance of science, the other the decay of religion, which have resulted in all the old general questions becoming either technical or ridiculous. This process in the development of civilisation we each of us have to repeat in ourselves. I, for instance, came up as a freshman enjoying conversation and argument more than anything else in the world; but I have gradually come to regard it as of less and less importance, because there never seems to be anything to talk about except shop and people's private lives, neither of which is suited for general conversation. . . .

If I was to write a *Weltanschauung* I should call it not "What I believe" but "What I feel." This is connected with Wittgenstein's view that philosophy does not give us beliefs, but merely relieves feelings of intellectual discomfort. Also, if I were to quarrel with Russell's lecture,[1] it would not be with what he believed but with the indications it gave as to what he felt. Not that one can really quarrel with a man's feelings; one can only have different feelings oneself, and perhaps also regard one's own as more admirable or more conducive to a happy life. From this point of view, that it is a matter not of fact but of feeling, I shall conclude by some remarks on things in general, or as I would rather say, not things but *life* in general.

Where I seem to differ from some of my friends is in attaching little importance to physical size. I don't feel the least humble before the vastness of the heavens. The stars may be large, but they cannot think or love; and these are qualities which impress me far more than size does. I take no credit for weighing nearly seventeen stone.

[1] "What I believe."

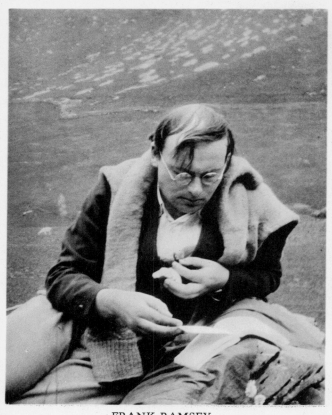

FRANK RAMSEY

Aged 25

(Austrian Tyrol, August, 1928)

My picture of the world is drawn in perspective and not like a model to scale. The foreground is occupied by human beings and the stars are all as small as threepenny bits. I don't really believe in astronomy, except as a complicated description of part of the course of human and possibly animal sensation. I apply my perspective not merely to space but also to time. In time the world will cool and everything will die; but that is a long time off still and its present value at compound discount is almost nothing. Nor is the present less valuable because the future will be blank. Humanity, which fills the foreground of my picture, I find interesting and on the whole admirable. I find, just now at least, the world a pleasant and exciting place. You may find it depressing; I am sorry for you, and you despise me. But I have reason and you have none; you would only have a reason for despising me if your feeling corresponded to the fact in a way mine didn't. But neither can correspond to the fact. The fact is not in itself good or bad; it is just that it thrills me but depresses you. On the other hand, I pity you with reason, because it is pleasanter to be thrilled than to be depressed, and not merely pleasanter but better for all one's activities.

February 28, 1925.[1]

[1] *Op cit.* p. 289-92.

REFERENCES

THE essays collected in this volume were first published (in
Great Britain) as follows:

I. SKETCHES OF POLITICIANS.

    1. "The Economic Consequences of the Peace" (November 1919), pp. 26-50.
    3. *The Nation and Athenaeum*, May 26, 1923.
    4. *The Nation and Athenaeum*, February 25, 1928.
    5. *The Nation and Athenaeum*, November 29, 1924.
    6. (i) *The Nation and Athenaeum*, March 5, 1927.
    6. (ii) *The Nation and Athenaeum*, March 9, 1929.
    7. *The Nation and Athenaeum*, April 28, 1928.
    8. *The Nation and Athenaeum*, March 27, 1926.

II. LIVES OF ECONOMISTS.

    2. *The Economic Journal*, September 1924.
    3. *The Economic Journal*, March 1926.
    4. (i) *The Economic Journal*, March 1930.
    4. (ii) *The New Statesman and Nation*, October 3, 1931.

INDEX OF NAMES

Printed in Great Britain by R. & R. CLARK, LIMITED, *Edinburgh*